Euripides, 3

Alcestis, Daughters of Troy,
The Phoenician Women,
Iphigenia at Aulis, Rhesus

Edited by
David R. Slavitt *a n d* Palmer Bovie

PENN

University of Pennsylvania Press
Philadelphia

Copyright © 1998 University of Pennsylvania Press

Printed in the United States of America on acid-free paper

10 9 8 7 6 5 4 3 2 1

Published by

University of Pennsylvania Press

Philadelphia, Pennsylvania 19104-4011

Library of Congress Cataloging-in-Publication Data

Euripides.
  [Works. English. 1997]
  Euripides / edited by David R. Slavitt and Palmer Bovie.
      p.   cm. — (Penn Greek drama series)
  Contents: 1. Medea. Hecuba. Andromache. The Bacchae—
2. Hippolytus. Suppliant women. Helen. Electra. Cyclops   3. Alcestis,
Daughters of Troy, The Phoenician Women, Iphigenia at Aulis, Rhesus
      ISBN 0-8122-3415-4 (v. 1: cloth : alk. paper).—ISBN 0-8122-1626-1
(v. 1: pbk : alk. paper).—ISBN 0-8122-3421-9 (v. 2 : cloth : alk. paper).—
ISBN 0-8122-1629-6 (v. 2 : pbk. : alk. paper).—ISBN 0-8122-3343-X
(v. 3 : cloth : alk. paper).—ISBN 0-8122-1650-4 (v. 3 : pbk. : alk paper)
      1. Euripides—Translations into English.   2. Greek drama (Tragedy)—
Translations into English.   3. Mythology, Greek—Drama.   I. Series.
PA3975.A1   1997
882'.01—dc21   97-28892
                                                                    CIP

Contents

Introduction by Palmer Bovie   vii

Alcestis   1
Translated by Fred Chappell

Daughters of Troy   61
Translated by Mark Rudman and Katharine Washburn

The Phoenician Women   137
Translated by Richard Elman

Iphigenia at Aulis   221
Translated by Elaine Terranova

Rhesus   313
Translated by George Economou

Pronouncing Glossary of Names   363

About the Translators   377

Introduction

Palmer Bovie

Classical Greek tragedy, which flourished in Athens during the fifth century B.C., grew out of country festivals originating a century earlier. Three different celebrations in honor of Dionysus, known as the rural Dionysia, occurred during the winter months. One of these, the Lenaea, was also observed at Athens in the sanctuary of Dionysus. In addition to song it offered ecstatic dances and comedy. Another, the Anthesteria, lasted for three days as a carnival time of revelry and wine drinking. It also included a remembrance of the dead and was believed to be connected with Orestes' mythical return to Athens purged of guilt for killing his mother Clytemnestra.

The rural Dionysia were communal holidays observed to honor Dionysus, the god of wine, of growth and fertility, and of lightning. Free-spirited processions to an altar of Dionysus were crowned by lyrical odes to the god sung by large choruses of men and boys chanting responsively under the direction of their leader. The ritual included the sacrifice of a goat at the god's altar, from which the term "tragedy," meaning goat-song, may derive. Gradually themes of a more serious nature gained ground over the joyful, exuberant addresses to the liberating god, legends of familiar heroes, and mythological tales of divine retribution. But the undercurrent of the driving Dionysiac spirit was seldom absent, even in the sophisticated artistry of the masterful tragic poets of the fifth century.

Initially the musical texts were antiphonal exchanges between the chorus and its leader. Thespis, who won the prize of a goat for tragedy at Athens in 534 B.C., is traditionally said to have been the first to appear as an actor, separate from the chorus, speaking a prologue and making set speeches, with his face variously disguised by a linen mask. A fourth festival, the City Dionysia or the Great Dionysia, was instituted by the ruler Peisistratus, also in 534, and nine years later Aeschylus was born. It seems that the major era of Greek tragic art was destined to begin.

The Great Dionysia, an annual occasion for dramatic competitions in tragedy and comedy, was held in honor of Dionysus Eleutheros. Its five-day celebration began with a procession in which the statue of Dionysus was carried to the nearby village of Eleutherai (the site of the Eleusinian Mysteries) and then back, in a parade by torchlight, to Athens and the precincts of Dionysus on the lower slopes of the Acropolis. In the processional ranks were city officials, young men of military age leading a bull, foreign residents of Athens wearing scarlet robes, and participants in the dramatic contests, including the producers (*choregoi*), resplendent in colorful costumes. The ceremonies ended with the sacrificial slaughter of the bull and the installation of Dionysus' statue on his altar at the center of the orchestra.

For three days each of the poets chosen for the competition presented his work, three tragedies and one satyr play (a farcical comedy performed in the afternoon after an interval following the staging of tragedies). In the late afternoon comedies were offered. The other two days were marked by dithyrambic competitions, five boys' choruses on one day, five men's on the other. The dithyramb, earlier an excited dramatic dance, became in the Athenian phase a quieter performance, sung by a chorus of fifty and offering little movement.

The theater of Dionysus at Athens was an outdoor space on the southern slope of the Acropolis. A semicircular auditorium was created on the hillside from stone or marble slabs, or shaped from the natural rock with wooden seats added. Narrow stepways gave access to the seats, the front row of which could be fitted out with marble chairs for official or distinguished members of the audience. From sites visible today at Athens, Delphi, Epidaurus, and elsewhere, it is evident that the sloping amphitheater had excellent acoustic properties and that the voices of the actors and the chorus were readily heard.

The acting area began with an *orchestra*, a circular space some sixty feet in diameter where the chorus performed its dance movements, voiced its commentaries, and engaged in dialogue with the actors. In the center of the orchestra was an altar of Dionysus, and on it a statue of the god. Behind the orchestra several steps led to a stage platform in front of the *skene*, a wooden building with a central door and doors at each end and a flat roof. The actors could enter and exit through these doors or one of the sides, retiring to assume different masks and costumes for a change of role. They could also appear on the roof for special effects, as in Euripides' *Orestes* where at the end Orestes and Pylades appear, menacing Helen with death, before she is whisked away from them by Apollo. The skene's facade represented a palace or temple and could have an altar in front of it. Stage properties included the *eccyclema*, a wheeled platform that was rolled out from the central door or the side of the skene to display an interior setting or a tableau, as at the end of Aeschylus' *Agamemnon* where the murdered bodies of Agamemnon and Cassandra are proudly displayed by Clytemnestra.

Another piece of equipment occasionally brought into play was the *mechane*, a tall crane that could lift an actor or heavy objects (e.g., Medea in her chariot) high above the principals' heads. This device, also known as the *deus ex machina*, was favored by Euripides, who in the climactic scene of *Orestes* shows Apollo protecting Helen in the air high above Orestes and Pylades on the roof. Or a deity may appear above the stage to resolve a final conflict and bring the plot to a successful conclusion, as the figure of Athena does at the end of Euripides' *Iphigenia in Tauris*. Sections of background at each end of the stage could be revolved to indicate a change of scene. These *periaktoi*, triangular in shape, could be shown to the audience to indicate a change of place or, together with thunder and lightning machines, could announce the appearance of a god.

The actors wore masks that characterized their roles and could be changed offstage to allow one person to play several different parts in the same drama. In the earliest period tragedy was performed by only one actor in counterpoint with the chorus, as could be managed, for example, in Aeschylus' *Suppliants*. But Aeschylus himself introduced the role of a second actor, simultaneously present on the stage, Sophocles made use of a third, and he and Euripides probably a fourth. From such simple elements (the orchestra space for the chorus, the slightly raised stage and its scene front, the minimal cast of actors) was created the astonishingly powerful poetic drama of the fifth-century Athenian poets.

What we can read and see today is but a small fraction of the work produced by the three major poets and a host of fellow artists who presented plays in the dramatic competitions. Texts of tragedies of Aeschylus, Sophocles, and Euripides were copied and stored in public archives at Athens, along with Aristophanes' comedies. At some later point a selection was made of the surviving plays, seven by Aeschylus, seven by Sophocles, nine by Euripides, and ten others of his discovered by chance. In the late third and early second centuries B.C., this collection of thirty- three plays was conveyed to the great library of Alexandria, where scholarly commentaries, *scholia*, formed part of the canon, to be copied and transmitted to students and readers in the Greco-Roman cultural world.

Euripides (485 – 406 B.C.) was born near Athens, the son of prosperous middle-class parents. He spent most of his life in study and in writing his poetry "in a cave by the sea in Salamis." At Athens his associates included Archelaus, a pupil of the philosopher Anaxagoras, Protagoras, Prodicus, and Socrates. Such acquaintances, cited by early biographers, are well worth considering in view of Euripides' flair for weaving philosophical debates into many dramatic dialogues, or marshaling logical principles in set speeches. During the oppressive decades of the Peloponnesian War, Euripides may have incurred the hostility of his fellow citizens by his denunciation of war and its havoc, a recurrent theme in many of his plays. For whatever reason, he withdrew into retirement, living a rather unsociable existence. For his conventional treatment of mythological figures and situations he was mercilessly mocked by the comic poets, especially Aristophanes. And his skeptical approach to standard religious conceptions may have disturbed many of his listeners. Late in life, three or four years before his death, Euripides left Athens for residence, first, in Magnesia and then in Macedon at the court of King Archelaus, where he was received with great honor. There he continued writing plays, his last work being *The Bacchae*, a dramatic limning of the dire consequences of abandoning belief in Dionysus.

Euripides differs from his fellow playwrights in several ways. He adopts unusual versions from the repertory of myth, and his plots and characters are often so realistically developed as to seem new and modern rather than classical. Often we see his principals escape from their predicaments. Fate turns out to be the unexpected. The chorus may interact with the players or its lyrics may form a descant on themes quite separate from the action in progress. In the fluent and quick-witted play of ideas, skepticism can override belief and logic and challenge simple convictions.

His *Electra* varies from the versions of Aeschylus and Sophocles in its astonishing recharacterization of Electra as now married to a peasant farmer who treats her with respect and honors her chastity. Their simple country hut becomes the scene of Clytemnestra's murder. Electra summons her mother on the pretext of having borne a child and wanting her there to perform the ritual of cleansing. With this ironic, macabre embellishment on the conventional murder scene, Euripides seems to be actually increasing the guilt felt by the children. But until this point Electra's conduct as the humble helpmeet of a husband with a heart of gold outclasses her mourning. She smolders with resentment but bides her time, waiting for Orestes, hoping. That Euripides sees her in a different light is also signaled in his refuting the others' recognition tokens. A lock of hair, a scrap of child's clothing, footprints? absurd to think of such things as clues to Orestes' identity! What he can be known by is the scar on his forehead, "on his brow—where he was cut in a fall, chasing a fawn with you in his father's courtyard" (ll. 568–69). So tangible and realistic a memory convinces Electra. The fact is that Orestes is scarred for life. His identification was not just a clever bit of literary criticism.

Brother and sister are, at the end of the *Electra*, brought to the depth of sorrow by the realization of what they have done. But they are lifted out of despair by the timely appearance of their divine relatives Castor and Polydeuces, *ex machina*. The Dioscuri, the heavenly Twins, have paused as they "speed to seas off Sicily, to protect the ships in danger there" (ll. 1335–36). Athens had sent an expedition to the aid of the fleet in Sicily in 413, so it appears that Euripides is being historical as well as mythical here. Electra is to leave Argos and marry Pylades, to live in exile. Orestes must go to Athens and await trial at the Areopagus. The children's generation, marked by the ancient curse of violence on their house, has nevertheless emerged to survive. The Dioscuri (Castor and Polydeuces were the divine brothers of Helen and Clytemnestra) also report, almost casually, that Menelaus and Helen will attend to the burial rites for Clytemnestra and Aegisthus. They explain that Menelaus and Helen have recently arrived from Egypt. She, Helen, never went to Troy, they add laconically.

The year 412 saw the production of Euripides' drama *Helen*, which offers the counter-myth that Hermes had spirited Helen away to Egypt, substituting for her at Troy a phantom image. In Egypt she enjoyed the protection of the king, Proteus, during the ten years of the Trojan war, but after his death his son holds her hostage and wants to make her his wife. She fends him off by maintaining a constant vigil at Proteus' tomb, a sacred refuge. This story line, sketched in by Helen in the prologue in her play, was suggested earlier by an episode in Book II, the Egyptian book, of Herodotus' *Histories*, and poems in praise of Helen by Stesichorus and other sixth-century lyric poets in Euripides' combination. He has seized the opportunity to dramatize Helen's rescue, starting with her joyful reunion with Menelaus, who has been shipwrecked with his crew and the phantom Helen on these shores. Her meeting with him surely constitutes the most appealing recognition scene of any in the Greek drama we know, and Euripides weaves a spell of exciting suspense as husband and wife devise the strategy for eluding their Egyptian captor. Plans are made and discarded until finally Helen hits on the right tactics, saying (almost under her breath) that even a woman might have "a good suggestion" (l. 1086). Their daring plan enables husband and wife to escape from impending doom, and Helen from captivity and slander.

Another Euripidean heroine to escape from peril is found in *Iphigenia in Tauris*. Orestes and Pylades join forces with Iphigenia in devising a plan to outwit the barbarous king of Thrace and sail away to Athens. The men supply the force, the woman the strategic plan. Men may be forceful, Euripides implies, but women are more resourceful. In other female figures, like Ion's mother in the *Ion* and Alcestis in the *Alcestis*, women are rescued from tragedy. Alcestis, indeed, is wrested from the arms of Death by Heracles and restored to her husband's embrace.

Euripides explores the complex dimensions of female character from many angles. In plays from the Trojan War cycle, women are towering figures of tragic sorrow as they voice the grief that descends on the victims of war. Swept up in the grotesque futility of war, the Trojan women endure further humiliation in the senseless murders of their children in the war's catastrophic aftermath. Small wonder that we should weep for Hecuba. A later representation of Andromache finds her married to Neoptolemus, Achilles' son, and having borne a son to him. As if this irony were not insult added to injury, Andromache is now threatened with murder by the new mistress who has replaced her. She is protected by Peleus (a Trojan Woman saved by a Trojan Man), but Menelaus and Hermione, the new mistress, are still bent on doing her in. At the melodramatic moment, Orestes arrives on the scene and will despatch Neoptolemus, taking Hermione as his bride. Here Euripides has ingeniously rescued two women from imminent destruction, one Trojan and one Greek, Hermione being the daughter of Helen. He evidently found such figures as the poignant Andromache and the jealousy-ridden rival Hermione well worth close attention.

The poet's fascinating portraits of celebrated women drawn from the mythological traditions rises to the level of Aeschylean or Sophoclean theatricality. While he may not invoke the grandeur of Aeschylus' vision or the nobility of Sophocles' unerring judgment, Euripides offers his audience real life human beings, natural characters under, at times, supernatural pressures. His memorable women Medea and Phaedra become avenging forces and are demonically driven to destroy the source of their happiness. They do not gain wisdom through suffering, but plunge into darkness. Medea may fly off to Athens in a chariot drawn by dragons, but in reality her burden is her murdered children and all she and Jason once cherished. Her husband is ruined: she, almost worse, is deluded. What she said of herself turns out to be true: "My will is stronger than my reason." Phaedra's psychological burden in the *Hippolytus* is shame and guilt. Her lust humiliates her and compels her to bring disgrace on the innocent young hero. His devotion to Artemis conflicts with her subjection to Aphrodite: both Hippolytus and Phaedra are destroyed in the clash of wills. Tragedy is, of course, the truth realized too late: and too late Theseus discovers his son's innocence and his wife's aberration.

From a terrifying view of women driven to a demonic state we find, in *The Bacchae*, Euripides' last play, what can be considered a misogynist stance. But on the whole this brutal drama chiefly brings to mind the peril of denying an underlying neutral power, the life force that of necessity controls all beings. That is, Dionysus, whose cosmic energy animates life and whose passionate powers motivate the "drama," the forward motion registered by Greek tragedy.

Toward men as heroes Euripides' attitude is sometimes disparaging. The men in *Iphigenia at Aulis* are hardly impressive as they assemble to sail against Troy. Only Achilles achieves some stature, and all are far below the unblemished radiance of Iphigenia, their victim. And Orestes, in the tragedy named after him, is frantic, haunted by his guilty conscience; he plunges wildly into futile gestures of revenge. Heracles can be driven mad and returns to his senses, chastened but none the wiser. In the first play of which we have a record, the *Alcestis*, produced at Athens in 438 B.C. and winner of second prize in the contest at the Great Dionysia, Euripides plays woman against man, wife against husband. The drama itself was in fact the fourth of the group offered, in place of a satyr play. But it does not function as a satyr play; rather, it sets the stage for a reconciliation of an ordinary man and his extraordinary wife. Alcestis has offered to die in her husband's stead, and it is only when Death leads her off the stage that her husband Admetus realizes what he has lost by his wrongminded acceptance of Alcestis' sacrificial gesture. Luckily, Heracles has come to visit his friend Admetus, who, in his characteristically hospitable manner, receives him cordially and hides his knowledge of Alcestis' death. But Heracles learns the truth and it is not too late: he strides off to confront Death, wrests Alcestis from the fatal grasp, and leads back a veiled female figure. He places her in Admetus' hands, instructing his host not to raise the veil until three days have passed. The bulky hero leaves. The play ends. We realize that this well-intentioned but blundering man and his somber, self-denying wife were well worth being saved from their tragic destiny, as the chorus exits, singing:

> The Powers take on many shapes;
> the gods accomplish miracles.
> What was predicted fails to happen,
> then gods reveal their hidden design:
> and this was what took place.

Alcestis

Translated by
Fred Chappell

Translator's Preface

Euripides' *Alcestis* is a difficult play, and it is not likely that my ignorance will enlighten problems that long centuries of learning have left unresolved. Its classification—as tragedy, comedy, tragicomedy, or satyr play—has been closely and inconclusively debated. The one fact rarely denied is that it is a lively and effective stage piece. For that reason, my main aim has been to make it playable. After that, I sought faithfulness, first to the spirit of the play as best I understood it, then to its text as best I could read it.

To make it playable, I've taken certain liberties, especially with the Chorus. They are traditionally identified simply as the Elders of Pherae, but I have dared to imagine them to be a troupe, or club, of professional mourners, though I am well aware that this function is in fact always in the charge of women. But such a role would not be inconsistent with their duties as responsible citizens and would help underline and account for the ritualized histrionic tone of both their mourning and that of Admetus. Ritual mourning is not to be judged by contemporary standards of "sincerity." I've also given the Chorus two leaders (First and Second Mourner) and allocated to them lines best read solo in this translation.

Alcestis is notorious, too, for its violent clashes of tone: tragedy, satire, sarcasm, gaiety, and buffoonery are recklessly but cunningly intermingled. So cunning, in fact, is Euripides' meld that heterogeneity turns out—under examination—to be homogeneous. The closest modern analogy I can think of is Richard Strauss' opera, *Ariadne auf Naxos*, in which a farcical framework gradually disappears into first a tragic, then a romantic, transcendent overview. *Alcestis* works just the other way; comedy triumphs over pathos—and bathos too, for that matter.

The necessity, then, is to get one part to flow into the next as smoothly as possible. So I have done away with acts and scenes and have identified the episodes with musical names (antiphonias, solos, duets, trios) and have given them musical tempo markings as aids to readers and actors in setting and modulating the tones of these episodes. These markings are suggestions at best and may easily be overlooked. They are only stage directions in shorthand. For example, when Admetus and his father Pheres begin with grave accusations a quarrel that ends in a spitting catfight, I wrote "andante, with gradual accelerando to allegro" rather than "The actors must start off deliberately and work with increasing heatedness and speed into a squabble, becoming more and more childish as they trade insults and reveal their innate cowardice." Musical marking seemed a way to point directions without psychologizing.

But I have been unable to find an overall voicing that might echo Euripides, whose language retains dignity without stiffness even in embarrassing scenes and who purposely includes both maudlin bathos in Eumeles' farewell to his mother and clownish slapstick with the drunken Heracles. I have tried and I have failed—yet I have failed in good company. Neither Richmond Lattimore, nor William Arrowsmith, nor Dudley Fitts and Robert Fitzgerald together could do justice to this odd but compelling drama. My favorite bête noir is Arthur S. Way in the Loeb edition; he translates two of Admetus' lines (551–52) thus: "Nay, verily: mine affliction so had grown / No less, and more inhospitable were I!" This is by no means his most outlandish effort. My version reads: "Of course not. My misfortune would not lessen / and I would merely be rudely ungracious." My lines may be tame but I believe them to be in English. In fact, I have generally striven for plain diction throughout, surmising that this gives the lines more speed and forward thrust than a more ornate style would allow. If *Alcestis* falters in tempo it will cease to dazzle; it will disintegrate to parts that make no whole. I labored to avoid that catastrophe.

As for sets and properties: The poet underscores with his first words (*O domat' Admetei*) the importance of Admetus' palace domicile and refers to it often in the play, so it should be more than a backdrop. It must be imposing. Before it stands a wall with big strong gates; the action takes place in the space before the wall. This space should be bare except for the properties the text requires—a couch for Alcestis, for example. Care should be taken with the wardrobe in order to get the mourning-ritual clothing correct. Heracles should probably be accoutered with his traditional lionskin and club, though the latter mustn't look silly. It's not a shillelagh, nor is it a comic-strip version of a weapon.

One of my favorite literary figures is the pulp-fiction writer Frederick Faust, who under his frequent pen name Max Brand invented Dr. Kildare and authored *Destry Rides Again*. When drunk he would bellow the Greek of Aeschylus and belligerently proclaim: "No gentleman reads Euripides!" Perhaps his own dull poetry indicates that he resented the "impurity" of Euripides' vision.

Yet if he had pondered *Alcestis* he might have remarked strong similarities between this story and his own western yarns. The play begins with outside rival factions, Apollo and Death, vying for control over the fate of a powerful local family. Death holds a mortgage (literally, a "death-debt") and the family is collapsing under the pressure of his demand. Then a lonesome wanderer, strong and well armed and immediately recognizable by his costume, arrives by accident. When his host family's predicament captures his attention, he vows to aid them in their plight. He wins the day. Then he rides off into the sunset, toward a new and equally dangerous adventure.

This story is always a jolly one in its basic outline, and Euripides understood that the inherent limitations preventing it from being a full-blooded tragedy of the Sophoclean type were at the same time dramatic strengths. There is something reassuring—even comforting—about a story in which we can pull for the hero with full confidence that he is going to triumph. The inevitabilities of tragedy are cleansing, but the improbabilities of romance are cheering. It is clear from the bitterly satiric scene between Admetus and his father, and from the cheeky, teasing final scene of the play, that the playwright was not taking his material with undue solemnity.

Alcestis has become, by the time it ends, a lighthearted variation on the tragic format. This fact does not make it a less serious play than, say, *Prometheus Bound*, for the themes it broaches are pressing and enduring. They are restated in masterly fashion in the medieval play of *Everyman*. But Euripides knew how to keep the profundity of his themes in the mind of his audience while at the same time both tweaking and coddling their expectations. And this is a main reason the play produces such mordant pleasure, as bittersweet as a Seville orange.

Cast

APOLLO, the god
DEATH
CHORUS OF ELDERS OF PHERAE, a mourning troupe
FIRST MOURNER
SECOND MOURNER
HANDMAID
ALCESTIS, wife of Admetus
ADMETUS, king of Pherae
EUMELUS, son of Admetus and Alcestis
HERACLES, son of Zeus and Alcmene
SERVANT
PHERES, father of Admetus
NONSPEAKING
    Daughter of Admetus and Alcestis
    Attendants
    Funeral procession

APOLLO
    This the palace of King Admetus:
                                    Here I,
    the god Apollo, consent to eat the food
    of common men, and this because of Zeus
    who thunderstruck my son Asclepius,
    killing him. In fury then I slaughtered
    the Cyclopes who fashioned Zeus' weapons.
    He forced me to atone by hiring on
    as menial labor for a mortal man.
    To Thessaly then I came, to tend the oxen
    of my host Admetus and to protect   10
    his holdings until this hour. I am a just god
    and recognize just men; Admetus, the son
    of Pheres, I then encountered and him I saved

from Death, deceiving the Three Fates, who promised
Admetus should not die if some one person
would take his place instead and die for him.
He went to everyone he knew as friend—
his father, and aged mother who gave him birth;
and only his wife Alcestis would agree
to die for him, forsaking the light of day.   20
Right now, inside this house, she languishes
in his arms. She breathes her last; the hour
appointed has arrived and she must die
and live no longer. Of this loved house I take
my leave that Death may not pollute me . . .

                                  He comes,
the Leader who will guide her down to Hades.
He's kept close watch upon her fatal day.
(Enter Death.)

Duet (allegro ma non troppo)

DEATH

What are you doing here?
Apollo here before the palace?
Apollo in this selfsame city?   30
Would you break again the laws,
transgress the boundaries hell-gods
have set? Were you not satisfied
to cheat the Fates with a sneaky trick
and save Admetus from the death he owed?
Now you've drawn your bow to guard
Alcestis, the daughter of Pelias,
who pledged to die for her Admetus.

APOLLO

Don't worry—justice and straight talk I offer.

DEATH

If you were just you wouldn't need your bow.   40

APOLLO

    I only keep it with me out of habit.

DEATH

    But now your unjust habit aids this house.

APOLLO

    I feel the sorrow that my friend must feel.

DEATH

    And so you'd take from me this second victim?

APOLLO

    It wasn't with my bow I took Admetus.

DEATH

    He's in the Upper World—and not the Lower.

APOLLO

    Because he gives his wife, the one you come for.

DEATH

    The one I'll take down with me, down and down.

APOLLO

    Go ahead and take her. Could I persuade you—

DEATH

    to destroy the one I must? That is my duty.   50

APOLLO

    Oh no: kill only when that death is due.

DEATH

    I think I understand where this is leading.

APOLLO

Cannot Alcestis live to riper years?

DEATH

No, she cannot. My honor is at stake.

APOLLO

You may take one life only, young or old.

DEATH

The younger the victim, the greater is my honor.

APOLLO

If she died later, the funeral would be grander.

DEATH

Now you argue in favor of the richest people.

APOLLO

And now you too are talking like a lawyer.

DEATH

Wouldn't the wealthy pay to put off death?   60

APOLLO

And so you won't confer this single favor?

DEATH

No, I will not. You know the way I am.

APOLLO

Abhorred by men, and by the gods despised.

DEATH

You cannot have the thing that is not yours.

APOLLO

    Cruel though you are, you shall not triumph,
    for there shall come to Pheres' palace here,
    sent by Eurystheus, the king of Mycenae,
    a hero ordered to bring him back from Thrace,
    that land of icy winter, a chariot
    drawn by Diomedes' man-eating mares.   70
    In this house of Pheres' son, Admetus,
    he shall be welcomed and by main strength
    shall tear away from you Admetus' wife;
    and so you earn no gratitude from me
    for giving up the woman—only my hatred.

DEATH

    All your talk will get you nothing from me.
    Alcestis travels down to the house of Hades.
    Now I go to ready her sacrifice:
    she is consecrate to the Nether Gods
    when once this sword of mine has cut her hair.   80
(brandishes sword)

      Antiphonia (andante)

(Enter Chorus of professional mourners, old men.)

FIRST MOURNER

    Why is this courtyard quiet now?
    Why silent the palace of Admetus?

SECOND MOURNER

    He has no friend here to announce
    if I must mourn the departed queen
    or if she still sees light of day,
    this daughter of Pelias, Alcestis,
    who all know as the finest woman
    that ever had a man for husband.

CHORUS
    Can you hear the sounds of sorrow,
    moaning, sighing,   90
    beating of hands,
    the rooms echoing lamentation?
    Not a single maidservant stands
    at the gate.
    O Paean, god of healing, come,
    turn back this flood tide of misfortune!

SECOND MOURNER
    No sound of crying . . . She still lives.

FIRST MOURNER
    She's but a corpse.

SECOND MOURNER
                    She's in her chamber.

FIRST MOURNER
    What gives you hope when I have none?

SECOND MOURNER
    Would Admetus inter, alone   100
    and unattended, so dear a wife?

CHORUS
    The spring-water jar for washing the dead
    is not seen standing at the gateway;
    nor is the ceremonial shorn
    lock of hair laid at the portal;
    nor is there sound of the servant girls
    beating their foreheads with their hands.

SECOND MOURNER
    And yet this day is the day appointed—

FIRST MOURNER
    Don't say—

SECOND MOURNER
            she must be laid in earth.

FIRST MOURNER
    You have pierced my soul with hurt.   110

SECOND MOURNER
    The longtime friend of a beloved person
    must weep, must weep in sorrow
    when that person is brought to ruin.

CHORUS
    Useless to send the sacred ships
    to Lycia or to dusty Ammon's
    temple; nothing will return
    to rescue pitiable Alcestis
    or bring her back. The fateful day
    has come. Useless to heap the altars
    of any god with handsome gifts.   120
    But once upon a time . . . If only
    he still gazed upon the light—
    Asclepius, son of the god
    Apollo, could draw Alcestis back
    from the domain of shadow, from
    the portals of the underworld.
    For he was able to raise the dead
    before the bolt that Zeus delivered
    killed him . . . But now what hope is there
    to hold out for Alcestis' life?   130
    Admetus has made all sacrifice,
    every altar runs with blood,
    but nothing remedies this evil.
(Enter handmaid.)

FIRST MOURNER
  But here, from out the house, a handmaid comes,
  all teary-eyed. What news will she bring me?
(addresses her)
  You cannot help but weep when master and mistress
  are sorrowing, but still we need to know
  whether Alcestis lives or if she's dead.

Antiphonia (andante ma non troppo)

HANDMAID
  The truth is that she's both alive and dead.

FIRST MOURNER
  How can the same be dead yet see the light?   140

HANDMAID
  She shudders on the farthest verge of life.

FIRST MOURNER
  The noble king must lose the noblest queen.

HANDMAID
  He cannot know his grief till it is on him.

FIRST MOURNER
  Is there no hope her life may yet be saved?

HANDMAID
  This is the day assigned to be her last.

SECOND MOURNER
  Are all things being done that need be done?

HANDMAID
  The robes that she'll be buried in are ready.

SECOND MOURNER
 Make known to her that she departs in glory,
 by far the greatest of women beneath the sun.

HANDMAID (*andante con moto*)
 The greatest—yes! Could anyone say different?   150
 How can she not be greater than all others?
 How much more could she show her loyalty
 than in giving up her own life for her husband's?
 This situation all the city knows of,
 but you'll be startled to hear what she has done.
 For when she knew this last day had arrived
 she bathed her glowing skin with river water
 and took her gowns and gems from the cedar chests
 and richly dressed herself, then took her place
 before the household and offered up a prayer: 160
(*changing the timbre of her voice*)
 "I go, O Hestia, to the underworld;
 and so I pray to you this final time.
 Protect my orphaned son and daughter:
 let him find a comely wife and her
 a noble husband. Let them live long lives,
 not dying early, as their mother dies.
 Let them live lucky, happy in their own country."
(*resuming normal voice*)
 All the altars in the house she visited,
 hung them about with garlands, and then prayed,
 and clipped the boughs of myrtle without a tear,   170
 without a moan. Nor did the fate upon her
 dim the healthy color of her face.
 She went then to the great bedchamber, flung
 herself upon the bed, and wept, and said:
(*changing timbre*)
 "O marriage bed, where I first lay unclothed
 for him that I shall die for, farewell. Farewell.
 I cannot hate you though I am doomed for you.

I would not fail Admetus nor his bed,
and yet another bride shall come to you,
though not more faithful—only luckier."   180
(resuming her own voice)
On her knees she kissed the bed and sprinkled
her tears upon it, and having wept her last,
she rose reluctantly and tried to leave,
and then came back, and many times went out
and many times returned to fling herself
upon the bed.
                    Her children clutched her dress
and cried; she hugged them tight and petted them
each one in turn, as a dying woman does.
And all the servants in the palace wept
in sympathy with their mistress. She touched the hands   190
of each of them, the lowest not excluded,
and spoke to them and listened to all reply.

All this, the misery of Admetus' house.
If he had died he only would have died;
but cowardice makes his life long agony.

SECOND MOURNER
And does Admetus not lament this sorrow,
since he must lose the noblest of all wives?

HANDMAID
He cries, and hugs his dear Alcestis close,
begging her never to abandon him,
though that's not possible. She fails, grows lighter   200
in his arms, can scarcely draw a breath—
yet tries and tries to look into the sunlight,
for she shall never see again the Sun
in its whole orbit and its shining splendor.
I will go now and report your presence.
Not all subjects support unfortunate kings
but you're a longtime friend of both of them.

Choral Interlude (allegretto con alcuna licenza)

FIRST MOURNER

O Zeus, is there no end to our masters' sorrow?
Is there no surcease from these dooms, these linked oppressions?

SECOND MOURNER

Will no one come out? Is it time   210
to cut my hair in mourning,
to wear the ritual's dark peplum?

FIRST MOURNER

O friends, it must be true—and yet
let us to the gods still give prayers.
The gods have strength unbounded.

CHORUS

O Paean, our god of healing, deliver
some respite to Admetus' suffering.
Our prayer grant us, oh grant us, we pray.
Formerly you found some aid;
oh, now again shield away Death,   220
keep back the blood-dripping Hades!

FIRST MOURNER

O O O O—the sorrow, the sorrow . . .
Admetus, son of Pheres,
your long pain begins with Alcestis' loss.

SECOND MOURNER

For these dread woes should he
not fall upon his sword,
not hang himself between
the sky and the unsteady earth?
His dear, his dearest one,
this day he shall see dead,   230
Her soul trembling in shadow.

FIRST MOURNER
    Oh see, oh see,
    Alcestis comes from the house with Admetus:

CHORUS
    Cry out, O land of Pheres:
    She is dying: this greatest woman
    Wanes away to Hades.

FIRST MOURNER
    Never again shall I aver that joy
    instead of sadness resides in marriage.
    For I remember the old times past,
    and now observe the condition of Admetus,   240
    his losing the paragon of wives.
    From this time forth he lives in pain.
(Enter Admetus and Alcestis, accompanied by attendants, their daughter,
and Eumelus their son.)

                    Duet (largo)

ALCESTIS
    O Sun, O bright and dazzling light of day!
    O clouds, white clouds wheeling across clear skies!

ADMETUS
    The sun looks down upon us both, both scourged,
    who have disserved no gods, deserve no death.

ALCESTIS
    O my country, my tall palace-home,
    My bridal bed—O Iolcas, my own country—

ADMETUS
    Gather your strength, my sad one, do not go
    from me. Pray the Powers to take pity.   250

ALCESTIS *(con moto)*
    I see the boat with its two oars
    upon the lake, and Charon, who
    ferries the dead across, one hand
    upon an oar, cries out to me,
    "Don't dawdle! Come on! You're holding me up!"
    He urges me with an angry tone.

ADMETUS
    This ferrying you speak of is hateful to me.
    O my unlucky one, how we must suffer.

ALCESTIS
    He takes me—he is taking me
    away—do you not see him now?—   260
    to the Palace of the Darkworld that
    winged Hades shadows, eyes
    staring from beneath murk brows—
    Stop, stop!—In this journey
    I am a woman god-deserted.

ADMETUS
    It is so painful to those who love you, most
    of all to me and to our grieving children.

ALCESTIS
    Let go of me, let go . . . Let me
    lie down. My feet are giving way.
    Hades is very near.   270
(stretches out on couch)
    The night closes over my eyesight.
    O children, O my children, your mother
    no longer is with you. Farewell,
    my children. Live in the happy light.

ADMETUS

    How dreadful! To hear your anguished speech,
    more painful even than death itself.
    I beg you, by the name of the gods,
    not to desert me, and by our children
    whom you orphan, to bear up.
    In your death is my Nothingness,   280
    in your love that we revere
    we have our life and love for one another.

       Solo (andante maestoso)

ALCESTIS *(calmly, recovering her senses)*
    You understand, Admetus, how I suffer;
    before I die I'll tell you my desire:

    to give you honor, your place in the sunlight,
    I am content to die. And yet I might
    have married another countryman and dwelt
    quite happily in the palace of a king.
    But torn away from you I would not live
    with my two orphans. I did not reserve   290
    the treasure of my youth; the man who fathered you
    and she who was your mother gave you over
    when the time was fit for them to die,
    fit for them to make a famous sacrifice
    for their son. Their only son you were;
    they had no hope for others once you were gone.
    and then the both of us could live long lives,
    and you would not lament your lonely state
    and how you must bring up motherless children.
    A god has caused these things. Let them then happen: 300
    so be it.
           Remember what is due to me—
    somewhat, I mean, for nothing can repay
    the loss of life . . . As you too will agree,

a just man loving our children as I do.
They must have their full authority:
do not remarry; do not install another
with a jealous heart, a cruel stepmother
to abuse them. Please, I beg you. *Please.*
More venomous than snakes, a new stepmother
detests the first wife's children. The father   310
stands a wall of strength and to his son
will always listen and give sound reply.
But, O my daughter, where is your happy girlhood?
How would the new stepmother deal with you?
She would ruin your marriage early on
by spreading vicious rumors. You'd have no mother
to give your hand in marriage, to comfort you
in childbirth as only gentlest mothers can.

For I must die. And not tomorrow, not
the day after tomorrow, comes this fate;   320
but *now* will I be numbered among the absent.

Goodbye. Take care. O husband, you may proclaim
your wife was noblest, and you, my children, you
may tell how truly noble your mother was.

SECOND MOURNER
    Be assured. I can promise for him
    he'll do these things unless he runs stark mad.

      Solo (andante)

ADMETUS
    As you say things must be, so shall they be.
    Don't be fearful on that score. Living,
    my one wife you were; my one wife dead.
    No Thessalian bride will call me husband;   330
    none has so great a sire, so fair a face.

Since we must lose our happiness in you,
now I look to find it in our children,
and pray the gods I shall—they are enough.
(*accelerando*)
Not for one year only will I mourn,
but for every final day I live.
My mother and my father I shall hate;
with words alone they loved me, not with deeds.
You saved my life by ransoming the dearest
things that you could have. Shall I not grieve,   340
having lost a wife like you?
(*allegretto con moto*)
                                        No parties,
no grand dinners, no flowers and no music—
all that used to gladden the palace shall cease.
I will not place my hand upon the lyre,
I will not cheer myself, singing to flutes
of Libya—you take from me all happiness.
Formed by the knowing hands of artists, your likeness
shall be laid out upon our marriage bed;
I shall take it in my hands and hold it close
and call your name as if I held you, holding   350
you not, believing my dear one in my arms:
a chilly pleasure, as I recognize,
yet it may cheer me. Often to my dreams
perhaps you'll come to soothe me, for those we love
we love to see in dreams in the swift nighttime.
(*tempo alla marcia; tempestoso*)
Oh, if I had the tongue, the music of Orpheus,
so I could charm Persephone and Hades
the king, her husband, bringing you back from Hades,
I would journey down. Hades' hellhound
would not stop me, nor the Deliverer   360
of Spirits, Charon, till I restored your life
once more to light.

                    And you must wait for me
until I die, making ready our house there
where you will be with me. And I will order
myself laid away in the cedar coffin
side by side with you; for separate
from you who were the one faithful to me
I shall not ever be, even in death.

FIRST MOURNER
    And as your friend, I'll mourn in sympathy
    with you for her. Alcestis merits it.   370

        Duet (largo)

ALCESTIS
    O children, you have heard your father's vow
    never to set another wife in power
    over you, thus to dishonor me.

ADMETUS
    So have I promised and so will I do.

ALCESTIS
    And so receive the children from my hand.

ADMETUS
    From a belovèd hand I take loved gifts.

ALCESTIS
    To them, for me, now you must be the mother.

ADMETUS
    I shall, I must, since you are taken from them.

ALCESTIS
    Dear ones, I die when most I need to live.

ADMETUS
Oh, what shall I do when you abandon me?   380

ALCESTIS
Time will lighten you. The dead mean nothing.

ADMETUS
Take me—O God!—take me now with you!

ALCESTIS
Let one die for one other. That will suffice.

ADMETUS
O Demon, what a wonderful wife you steal!

ALCESTIS
My eyes grow dim, my eyelids heavier.

ADMETUS
If you leave me, woman, I am lost.

ALCESTIS *(ritardo)*
Say of me now that I am nothingness.

ADMETUS
Raise your head! Do not desert your children!

ALCESTIS *(morendo)*
I do not want to . . . But, children, this is goodbye.

ADMETUS
Oh look at them! Oh look!

ALCESTIS
                        I am nothing.   390

ADMETUS
>Are you leaving us?

ALCESTIS
>   Farewell.

ADMETUS
>   Oh no . . .

CHORUS
>Now she is gone. Admetus' wife is gone.

EUMELUS *(allegro)*
>I sorrow for myself. To earth
>my mother has gone down. O father,
>she lives amid sunlight no more.
>You have left to us the life
>of orphans. Look at her eyelids,
>look at her strengthless hands!
>Listen to me, O mother, listen—
>Mother . . . I . . . I . . . O mother . . .   400
>I am like your little pet bird
>that you gave kisses to—

ADMETUS
>She cannot hear. She cannot see. The worst
>has happened that could happen to all of us.

EUMELUS *(allegro)*
>Father, I'm too young to be
>abandoned lonely and adrift
>with no mother. Oh,
>how hard things are for me, for you,
>my sister, who must suffer this fate . . .
>O father . . .   410

Ruined, ruined is your marriage now.
You were not able to walk together
to the end of your years. She died first.

SECOND MOURNER
You must endure, Admetus, this disaster.
You're not the first nor will you be the last
among mankind to lose a noble wife.
All of us know that all of us must die.

ADMETUS
I know. This sorrow did not fall on me
unlooked for; I have lived in lengthy anguish.
(andante marcato)
But now I must prepare for burial rites: 420
you shall be there to echo my paean
to the unappeasable god of death.
Let all Thessalian men under my rule
take part in mourning this woman, cutting short
their hair and putting on their robes of black.
And you who rein four horses to the car
or bridle the one racer, take your blade
and shear their manes. And let there be
no sound of flute or lyre inside the city
until twelve months have passed, for I shall not   430
bury another who meant so much to me,
Another person who has loved me so.
she deserves all honor I can give
since she alone would ever die for me.
(Exeunt, with Alcestis' corpse borne off.)

> *Antiphonia (allegretto)*

FIRST MOURNER
O daughter of Pelias,
I bid you farewell in the palace of Hades,
in that place of darkness where you are.

Lord Hades, you must know
that Charon with his boat of double oars
never has and never will ferry to the shore   440
of Acheron a finer woman.

CHORUS

The muses' devotees
shall sing with the tortoise-shell lyre
and its seven strings a mourning song,
and Sparta shall sing hymns of you
all night beneath the high-sailing moon
when the seasons bring again the month
of Carneius. In Athens, too, the city
wealthy and fortunate, shall the singers
take you as subject for their songs.   450

SECOND MOURNER

If only I could have the strength
to deliver you back to the light,
bringing you out of the mazes of Hades,
through the currents of Cocytus, river
of lamentation, with Charon's oar!
For only you among all women,
You alone,
had courage to exchange your life
for your husband bound to the Darkworld.
May the earth lie light upon you, Alcestis.   460
And if Admetus brings another
to the bridal bed I shall despise him,
and his children shall despise him.
When for Admetus' sake
his mother would not die for him
nor his old father who gave him being,
when neither would ransom his life
though both were gray with years—
then you, in the quick of life,

gave up for him, and have abandoned daylight.   470
How happy my time would be if I
could be married to a wife so true:
But in this life they do not often appear.
(Enter Heracles accompanied by a servant.)

Trio (allegro spiritoso)

HERACLES

Strangers living here in the land of Pheres,
tell me if I find Admetus in.

SECOND MOURNER

Yes, Pheres' son is present, Heracles.
But tell us why you came to Thessaly,
stopping here at Pherae on your way.

HERACLES

A labor for Eurystheus, king of Tiryns.

FIRST MOURNER

Where are you headed? What task must you do?   480

HERACLES

A quest for Diomedes' four-horsed chariot.

FIRST MOURNER

But can you do it? Do you know this man?

HERACLES

I don't. I've never traveled the Bistonian country.

FIRST MOURNER

I think you'll have to fight to get those horses.

HERACLES

I've put myself in jeopardy before.

SECOND MOURNER
> What good would it do you to kill that king?

HERACLES
> Then I can bring the horses to Eurystheus.

SECOND MOURNER
> It won't be easy for you to bridle them.

HERACLES
> Still I can do it—if they don't breathe flames.

FIRST MOURNER
> But they chew men with their quick-biting jaws.   490

HERACLES
> Wild mountain animals eat so, not horses.

SECOND MOURNER
> You can see their mangers stained with blood.

HERACLES
> Who does the breeder of them name his father?

FIRST MOURNER
> Ares, lord of the golden shields of Thrace.

HERACLES *(chagrined, but then determined)*
> You tell me I must always climb sharp slopes,
> battling with Ares' sons, Lycaoön first,
> and then with Cycnus. Now in this third contest
> I must pit myself against the horses there,
> and against their master too. Even so,
> no man alive shall ever see the son   500
> of Alcmene back down from an enemy.

SECOND MOURNER
> But here now is the ruler of this country,
> Admetus coming out of the palace.

(Enter Admetus.)

Duet (allegro ma non troppo)

ADMETUS
> Greetings, son of Zeus, kinsman of Perseus.

HERACLES
> Greetings to Admetus, king of Thessaly.

ADMETUS
> I thank you, understanding your good will.

HERACLES
> Why have you shaved and put on mourning clothes?

ADMETUS
> My duty's to inter a corpse today.

HERACLES
> May the gods have kept your children safe!

ADMETUS
> My own begotten children are in the house.   510

HERACLES
> If your father died—well then, it was time.

ADMETUS
> Heracles, my father and mother live.

HERACLES
> Is it your wife Alcestis who has died?

ADMETUS
> In her regard I have to give two answers.

And deep in my heart I must believe
the reverent man will be rewarded.
(Enter funeral procession, with Pheres and his wife; Admetus addresses them.)

ADMETUS
    O gathering of Pherean comforters,
    now that the servants have prepared the body
    and bear it off to tomb and pyre, salute—
    as our custom tells us we should do—
    Alcestis as she travels her last journey.   600

FIRST MOURNER
    But now I see your father tottering forth,
    age-hobbled; his retinue is carrying
    clothing to Alcestis as the burial offering.

     Duet (andante, with gradual accelerando to allegro)

PHERES
    My son, I come to share your sorrowing;
    you've lost a noble and a virtuous wife,
    as no one will deny. But all these things
    must be endured, however difficult.
(offers bracelets to Admetus, who pushes them aside)
    Take these ornaments; let her go down
    into the earth. Her body must be cherished
    because, my son, she died to save your life;   610
    she left me with a child, not to be ruined
    by the undermining years without you—
    and so has given honor to all women
    by daring this high deed.
                   O savior-woman,
    who raised me from my fall a thousand thanks!
    may you find Hades peaceful.
                   And I proclaim
    this marriage worthy, worthless the other kind.

ADMETUS

    I did not invite you to this burial,
    nor do I think you come here as a friend.
    She will not wear these ornaments you bring.   620
    Nothing of yours can give her burial honor.
    You should have grieved when *I* was going to die,
    Yet then you stood apart. And now you weep?
    Are you not the father of my body?
    And did that woman who was called my mother
    give birth to me? Or was I fathered by a slave
    and secretly brought to wet-nurse with your wife?
    When you were tested, you showed what you are,
    so I believe that I am not your son.
    You are cowardly and lacking nerve,   630
    for, having come to life's last boundary,
    you had no will to die for me, no courage.
    To a stranger woman you left this task,
    and her only I will call my father and mother.

    A lovely thing you might have done in dying
    for your son; little time remained for you.
    But she and I would live our lives together
    and I alone would not lament my sorrows.
    You had the luck to be as happy as any:
    the best years of your life you lived a king   640
    and had me as an heir to your domain;
    you would never have died without issue,
    leaving your household as a prey to strangers.
    Nor could I say that I was disrespectful
    and so deserved to die, for I revered you
    above all else . . . And from my parents—such thanks!

    You'd better get some other sons—and quickly!—
    to tend you in declining years, perform
    the funeral rites and lay your corpse in state.
    This my hand will never bury you.   650

To you I am a dead man. I only live
because another kept me in the light.
I call myself *her* son, cherish *her* years . . .
Old men pretend to pray for death, tired out
with age and in the weary years of life.
But then when Death shows up, they change their minds—
old age no longer seems a burden to them.

CHORUS

Quiet! Present pains suffice. O son,
do not exasperate your father's spirit.

PHERES

O son, do you imagine you're quarreling with   660
cheap hired help from Lydia or Phrygia?
Understand that I am Thessaly stock,
my father Thessaly-born, all free and clear.
These words are but your childish insolence;
you cannot fleer at me, then run away.
I fathered you and trained you as the lord
of all these lands. But I won't die for you.
There is no ancient law of Greece that says
fathers are obliged to die for children.
Into your own life you are born, for good   670
or ill. From me you've gotten what is proper.
You rule many people; many broad acres
I leave to you, left by my father to me.
What is my crime? How did I steal from you?
Don't die for *me*—and I won't die for *you*.
You love the light. Can your father hate it?
I think we spend a long time underground
and life before is very short but sweet.

Shamelessly you plotted not to die;
you evaded fate by killing your wife, Alcestis.   680
You who call me a coward allowed a woman

to die for you, most cowardly child alive.
You've made a clever plan never to die,
bringing death on death to many wives;
and curse your friends when they don't fall for it,
when they turn down a coward like yourself.
(Admetus starts to speak but is silenced)
Quiet! You know how you love your life—
well, so do others. And if you call us names,
you'll hear names back that bear the ring of truth.

CHORUS

Your curses, Pheres, with those of Admetus,   690
are enough. Old man, don't insult your son.
(Allegro, accelerando to prestissimo as the scene continues.)

ADMETUS *(to Pheres)*

Keep on talking; you'll get back what you give.
You make a damnable mistake with me.

PHERES

To die for you would be a graver mistake.

ADMETUS

Do young men and old men die the same death?

PHERES

I think we live one life and never two.

ADMETUS

One life for you—if it's as long as God's!

PHERES

You curse your parents who have never wronged you.

ADMETUS

Long life—that's all you ever think about.

HERACLES

Why should I thirst because a stranger died?   790

SERVANT

This was a highly intimate concern.

HERACLES

Did he have troubles he didn't tell me of?

SERVANT

Take care of yourself. We'll care for him.

HERACLES

You don't sound like you're grieving for a stranger.

SERVANT

Correct. That's why I disapprove your drinking.

HERACLES

Have my hosts here not been straight with me?

SERVANT

You found a rotten hour to find welcome.
Everyone's in mourning. Look at my head
all shaved and my black robes.

HERACLES

                              Well then, who died?
One of the children? Or was it Father Pheres?   800

SERVANT

Stranger, it is Admetus' wife who died.

HERACLES

Really?—And yet you welcomed me inside?

SERVANT
>He'd be ashamed, to turn you out of doors.

HERACLES (*quickly sobering*)
>O Admetus! What a wife you've lost!

SERVANT
>All of us are lost—not only she.

HERACLES (*andante rubato*)
>I guessed so much, seeing his eyes all teary,
>his shaven head, his face. Yet he convinced me
>he was carrying a stranger to the grave.
>Against my better judgment I entered here
>and began carousing in the house of the man   810
>who cherishes guests. He must have been heartbroken.
>Shall I keep on drinking, wearing this flower wreath?
>You should have told me of the misery here.
>Where is he keeping her? Where can I find them?

SERVANT
>Beside the straight road leading to Larissa
>you'll find a handsome tomb outside the walls.
(*Exit servant.*)

Solo

HERACLES (*tempo alla marcia; maestoso*)
>Oh, my ravaged heart! . . . Now my hand
>must show that I'm the son who's born of Zeus
>by the daughter of Electryon, Alcmene,
>I have to save this woman who just died;   820
>to favor Admetus I'll bring Alcestis back.

>I'll watch for Death, the black-robed deadly lord;
>I'm sure I'll find him at the tomb, drinking
>the blood of sacrifice. If I can hide

and leap out on him, grab him in my arms,
and crack his ribs, no one can take him from me,
till he gives up the woman. And if I miss
my prey, if he does not come to the sacrifice
of blood, then I will journey down to visit
Persephone and Hades in their sunless halls.   830
I know that they'll let me deliver Alcestis
to Admetus, who did not turn me away
although he suffered a dreadful heartache
which his nobility kept secret from me.
Where is there a better host in Thessaly
or in all Greece? He shall not say he showed
his generosity to a churlish man.

(Enter Admetus with Chorus and funeral cortege.)

Antiphonia (andante troppo expressivo histrionic)

ADMETUS

O God . . . Detestable this view, this sight
of the house without Alcestis. O God, O God . . .
Where can I go or stay? What can I say   840
or do? Or never say and never do?
Why may I not die myself?
Why must I endure the evil luck
that is my twin my mother bore?
The dead I envy and would like
to share their palaces with them.
I take no pleasure in the light
of day or in walking upon the earth.
Death has taken my precious one
and given her over to Hades.   850

CHORUS

Go on, go on: into your house.

ADMETUS

O God.

CHORUS
> Your sorrows are our own.

ADMETUS
> > > O God . . .

FIRST MOURNER
> I know how deep your anguish is,
> I know.

ADMETUS
> > Oh, no.

SECOND MOURNER
> > > But wailing's no help.

ADMETUS
> O God, oh, no.

CHORUS
> > > Never to see again
> the face of your beloved—that's hard . . .

ADMETUS
> You recall my heartbroken grief.
> Can any hurt be worse for a man
> than the loss of such a wife? I wish
> I'd never married and shared my house.   860
> I envy the childless bachelors.
> They were responsible but for one
> existence and so could never suffer.
>
> The sickness of our little ones,
> or Death that ravages the bridal bed—
> too much to bear when we might live
> womanless, childless, to the end.

CHORUS
    Luck, hard Luck, has thrown you down.

ADMETUS
    O God.

CHORUS
            You cannot stop your grieving.

ADMETUS
                            No . . . no . . .

FIRST MOURNER
    You carry an enormous load,   870
    Yet still—

ADMETUS
            O God . . .

SECOND MOURNER
                    You're not the first—

ADMETUS
    Oh . . . oh . . .

CHORUS
                    —to lose a wife. Hard Luck
    destroys each man differently.

ADMETUS
    Oh, prolonged grief and sorrow
    for those belovèd under the earth.
    Why did you hold me back from throwing
    myself into the grave to lie
    forever with the noblest woman?
    Two souls, not just one, would fall

as prey to Hades, both souls faithful, 880
to cross together the underworld lake.

SECOND MOURNER

An only son who deserved deep mourning
was lost to one of my close kin,
and yet he bore the sorrow bravely,
though his hair was white, his years
advanced, and he had no son to prop him
in his weakness for the rest of life.

ADMETUS

O house, how can I enter you?
How can I shelter here since Luck
has turned its face from me? O God, 890
what changes have come upon all things!
Once, long ago, with Pelian torches
and bridal song, I entered here,
holding my loved one by the hand.

The revelers followed after us,
praising her who now is dead,
praising me for kingly birth-lines,
because we nobles had joined our lives.
But marriage hymns are lamentations;
my white robes now are changed to mourning, 900
and I return to an empty house
and to the bed of a hermit.

CHORUS

Suddenly a whelming grief has fallen
upon your happiness, a hard-considered
understanding. Even so,
your spirit and your life are safe.
Your wife has died, deserted your love.
What's new in this? Many times
Death has parted husbands and wives.

ADMETUS

    My friends, though others may think differently,   910
    it seems to me my wife's lot is the happier.
    She's found the end of her courageous pain;
    suffering shall not trouble her again.
    I should have died but am condemned to live
    a bitter life. At last I understand . . .
    How can I make myself enter this house?
    Whom would I greet with joy? Who could greet me
    with joy? And how should I comport myself?
    The loneliness within will drive me out;
    I'll see my wife's bed empty, vacant her chairs,   920
    all the rooms disordered, littered, my children
    clutching my knees and calling for their mother,
    the servants lamenting the mistress of the house.
    All this inside the house. In the world outside
    I shall be barred from marriage feasts and driven
    from the gatherings of our Thessalian women.
    I won't be able to look at my wife's friends,
    for they are of the same age that she was.
    My enemies will say, "There goes Admetus
    who was so afraid of death he caused his wife   930
    to die instead. What kind of man is that?
    He hates his parents, though he refused to die."

    This dreadful reputation is but one
    more burden. How can I live honorably,
    if I must live in misery and shame?

FIRST MOURNER *(andante maestoso)*

    I have accompanied the Muses
    and gone to the mountaintops;
    I have studied all the wisdom;
    but Fate is insuperable
    and nothing overcomes it: 940
    not the ancient Thracian tablets
    scored with the wisdom of Orpheus,

not the medicine that Apollo
taught to the school of Asclepius
to heal the diseases of mankind.
None visits the altars of Fate,
no one worships her statues,
she ignores the sacrifices.
Goddess, do not trouble
me now more than you've done   950
in the earlier part of life.
For though Zeus may pronounce,
the judgment proceeds from you.

CHORUS

The hardest metal gives way
to your force; the way of your will
knows not the slightest compassion.
With her hands like iron the goddess has seized you.

SECOND MOURNER

You must submit. Your tears can have no power
to bring the departed to life. Even the heroes,
the children of gods, faint in the darkness   960
of Death. Alcestis was dear when living
and still is dear in her place with the dead.
Your bedmate was always the noblest of women.

CHORUS

No longer we call it a tomb, the grave
where Alcestis is buried. Instead, it's a place
as holy as the fanes of the gods, saluted
by every traveler on the roadway.

SECOND MOURNER

The wanderer shall turn from the main road
and say, "She gave up her life for her husband.
Now she's become a powerful Spirit.   970
O goddess, look after us carefully."

CHORUS
> This is the way that men shall talk of her.

FIRST MOURNER
> But now it seems to me that Heracles
> is coming, Admetus, toward your house.

(Enter Heracles, with a veiled woman.)

> *Scene (allegro calmando; poi accelerando)*

HERACLES
> A friend should tell a friend what's on his mind,
> Admetus, instead of hiding what's in his heart.
> If I came here during your troubles, I'd expect
> to be able to show that I'm your friend.
> You didn't say it was your wife who died;
> as if you were mourning for a mere stranger,   980
> you took me in. I put a wreath of flowers
> upon my head and poured the gods libations
> while your house was filled with grief and mourning.
> It's you I hold responsible—*you*;
> even so, I won't complain against you.
> Let me tell you why I've come back here.
> Take this woman from me, guard her closely,
> until I've killed the tyrant of Bistonia
> and brought the Thracian horses along with me.
> If anything should happen to me—though   990
> I'm sure that nothing will—I'll give her to you
> as a servant to your house.
>   I had a hard time
> winning her. I ran across some games
> while traveling, athletic competitions
> open to all, and there I won this prize,
> this woman. Horses they gave for the easier sports;
> for boxing and for wrestling they gave beeves.
> Then they offered a woman. There I was:
> to miss that wonderful opportunity
> would be a shame. So, as I told you before,   1000

I give her to your care, my hard-won prize,
not something that I got by thievery.
Maybe one day you will thank me for it.

ADMETUS

Not to insult you, nor to make of you
an enemy, were reasons I concealed
Alcestis' fate. If you had gone elsewhere
for courtesy that would have been worse grief.
And I had trouble enough to occupy me.

This woman here—let me beg of you,
O prince—should be joined to the company   1010
of some Thessalian who is not in mourning.
My friends in Pherae will welcome you.
Do not bring back my grief. If I saw her
within the house I could not keep from crying.
Don't make my pain more painful; I suffer enough.
Where in the palace would a young girl stay?
Her clothes and ornaments tell me that she's young.
Could she live under one roof with the men?
Moving freely among them, could she stay chaste?
It's hard to rein the young in, Heracles,   1020
and it's your cause that I am thinking of.
Or could I lodge her in Alcestis' chamber?
How could I bear her occupying that bed?
I know that I'd be shamed for double reasons:
the people would say that I betrayed my wife
to gain the bed of another woman; Alcestis
herself, whom I must reverence, would blame me.

O woman, whoever you may be, you have
Alcestis' form, you have Alcestis' body . . .
Oh, oh . . . For God's sake, take her from my sight.   1030
Don't add insult to injury . . . I look
at her, she seems to be my wife . . . My heart

is breaking, my eyes are flooding with tears . . .
In misery I eat the salt of grief.

FIRST MOURNER

I cannot say your luck has gotten better—

CHORUS

We must bear what the gods visit upon us.

Duet (allegro, becoming presto giocoso)

HERACLES

If only I could bring Alcestis back
to the light of day from the dark kingdoms of earth,
I would give her to you as a present.

ADMETUS

I know you'd wish to, but it's to no purpose.   1040
The dead cannot return to the light of day.

HERACLES

Don't unman yourself. You must bear up.

ADMETUS

Some things are easier to say than do.

HERACLES

What good will it do you to weep forever?

ADMETUS

I know, I know. But my love has undone me.

HERACLES

Our love for the departed brings on our tears.

ADMETUS

More than I can say: I am destroyed.

HERACLES
You lost a noble wife. Who can deny it?

ADMETUS
For Admetus, then, no pleasure remains in life.

HERACLES
Time brings healing; now your grief is raw.   1050

ADMETUS
If Time is Death, then you may be correct.

HERACLES
You'll be consoled by wedding a new woman.

ADMETUS
Quiet! What madness are you speaking now?

HERACLES
Come now. You mean to sleep alone, unmarried?

ADMETUS
No woman living will share a bed with me.

HERACLES
And do you think the dead care much for that?

ADMETUS
Wherever she is, I must honor Alcestis.

HERACLES
Well, good for you. But folks will think you're cracked.

ADMETUS
Just as long as they don't call me Bridegroom.

HERACLES

I must admire your faithful love of her.   1060

ADMETUS

I'll be faithful unto death—or die trying.

HERACLES *(offers woman)*

In that case, take this woman into your house.

ADMETUS

No. By the god who fathered you: *Never*.

HERACLES

But if you fail to, you'll be doing wrong.

ADMETUS

And if I do, my heart will tear to pieces.

HERACLES

Give in. This pleasure might prove to be good luck.

ADMETUS

No . . . I wish you'd never won her in the ring.

HERACLES

When I triumphed—well, you also triumphed.

ADMETUS

Nicely said . . . And yet she ought to leave.

HERACLES

All right, she goes. But are you really sure?   1070

ADMETUS

I'm sure . . . I hope you won't be vexed with me.

HERACLES
But I've thought hard about what I am doing.

ADMETUS
All right, you win . . . But it's no fun for me.

HERACLES
Give in. One day you'll understand, believe me.

ADMETUS *(to attendants)*
Take her. It seems the house must welcome her.

HERACLES
This woman can't be placed in the care of servants.

ADMETUS
If that's the case, then lead her in yourself.

HERACLES
Not I. It's up to you to take her in.

ADMETUS
I will not touch her. Let her go alone.

HERACLES
I trust no other hand than your right hand.   1080

ADMETUS
O Prince, you impose on me against my will.

HERACLES
Put your hand out now and take the woman.

ADMETUS *(averts his face from her)*
I'll do it the way I would behead a gorgon.

HERACLES
> Got her?

ADMETUS
> Yes.

HERACLES
> Hold on. You'll thank this son
> of Zeus one day for the house-gift that he brought.
> *(raises veil on Alcestis)*
> Look and see. Does she look like your wife,
> or not? Let happiness end your long grief.

ADMETUS
> My God! What can I say? This miracle
> is beyond all hope! Is this my wife I see?
> Or a happy delusion the gods have sent?   1090

HERACLES
> No, no: it really is your wife you see.

ADMETUS
> But what if it's some phantom of the dead?

HERACLES
> Please don't think that I'm a spirit-medium.

ADMETUS
> But is this wife the same one that I buried?

HERACLES
> She is. How wonderfully your luck has changed!

ADMETUS
> A living wife that I can touch and talk to?

HERACLES

Speak to her. Your every wish came true.

ADMETUS

O darling wife! Sweetest face and figure!
Now I have you—I thought I never would.

HERACLES

She's yours. And may the gods never be jealous . . .   1100

ADMETUS

O best of all the sons of the great Zeus—
may your father bless you and keep you.
You alone have been my savior.
How did you bring her from Shadow into Light?

HERACLES

I fought against the Power who held her hostage.

ADMETUS

You mean to say you fought with Death himself?

HERACLES

I hid outside the tomb and wrestled him down.

ADMETUS

Why does my Alcestis stand so silent?

HERACLES

Before you hear her speak she must be freed
of her consecration to the gods of death: 1110
and that will happen in three days from now.
But go ahead and lead her in, Admetus,
and always keep your kindly ways to guests.
Take care! I've got to go and finish the jobs
that I contracted to do for Eurystheus.

ADMETUS
>Stay with us here awhile. Sit by the hearth.

HERACLES
>Someday soon . . . But now I must be running along.
(Exit.)

ADMETUS
>Good luck, my friend. Please call on us again.
(to Chorus)
>>Throughout the towns, the four quarters of the realm,
>>let choral hymns arise in festival, 1120
>>and barbecue the sacrificial oxen.
>>A better life awaits us than the one
>>that was the past. I call myself a happy man.

CHORUS *(allegro; piu beffardo)*
>>The Powers take on many shapes;
>>the gods accomplish miracles.
>>What was predicted fails to happen,
>>then gods reveal their hidden design:
>>and this was what took place.

Daughters of Troy

Translated by
Mark Rudman and
Katharine Washburn

Andromache's speech in lines 895 ff. and her ensuing dialogue with Hecuba are among the most sublime and rending utterances in all literature. This is an understatement. For what has preceded this is an act that can only be called unspeakable, unendurable. At one point in the play, the messenger Talthybius, caught in a double bind, fantasizes that the women are setting fire to their own tent, preferring suicide to existence under the yoke of the Greeks.

I mention an unutterable action. I should add that this is the only action in *Daughters of Troy*. The rest of the play is an oratorio: speeches, monologues with sparse dialogue and bits of stichomythia within jostle each other. To say this is to say that *Daughters of Troy* is a problematical play, but almost all of Euripides is problematical, especially in tone. As everyone knows, he is the last of the great triumvirate of tragedians; yet where Aeschylus and Sophocles deal with primal and eternal materials in a consistently "high" manner and stay on a sublime plane, Euripides is an ironist. Anyone can recognize that *Daughters of Troy* begins not long after the *Iliad* ends and is both commentary and continuation of Homer. Many of his lines play on lines by his two great forerunners, usually with a twist, usually with a slight element of parody. This—dare I call it?—archness poses special difficulties for translators.

Some of the longer speeches try one's patience. In this play I would single out Helen's monologue in defense of herself. Filled with rhetorical tropes, clichés, archaisms, it leaves no doubt as to her duplicity, which listeners at the time could identify. This effect is magnified by the way this glamorous creature appears amidst the smoke-blackened ruins. The play could have been called *Waiting for the Gods*, but the gods are no more responsive to being summoned here than they are in modern literature like *Waiting for Godot*. In her opening speech Hecuba says:

Dust and ash sting my eyes.
Our kingdom is come: to ruin.
The sea can swallow us.
I brace myself against the changing of the gods.
We near the narrows.
We have no say in what course the helmsman takes;
his face is covered. Was he ever our friend? (129–35)

In spite of the fact that we have many more plays by Euripides than by the other two, his oeuvre is little known, and only the *Bacchae, Iphigenia at Aulis,* and *Medea,* along with *Daughters of Troy,* form accidentally a sort of quartet. In reading various translations after I was first asked to translate *Daughters of Troy,* two very different ones stood out, like Scylla and Charybdis. I was already familiar with Edith Hamilton's readable version, which is often performed and was used in the Michael Cacayonnis film (with Katherine Hepburn as Hecuba and Vanessa Redgrave as Andromache): it has both the virtues and the limitations of a certain simplicity. More bedeviling, Richmond Lattimore's version is a poem, accomplishing many high rhetorical tropes and skillful solutions to the meanings embedded in the Greek. Why, then, do another version of the play at all? I found it difficult to visualize his lines being spoken on stage.

Perhaps it was the very shapelessness of the play's structure that provided a certain challenge. I wanted to make it taut, fast, and playable, and give it the quality of living speech. It was a stroke of fortune to see an earlier version, done in collaboration with the classicist Diskin Clay, performed at the University of Virginia. Afterward, I knew my instinct to keep the play spare was right: a lot happened in the silences, the pauses, the moments in between. The physical presence of the actors created its own dialectic.

At times in the play, speech achieves an almost universal language of mourning. After the unutterable happens, Andromache's son Astyanax (the name means "lord of the city") is hurled over the battlements, her speech moves almost beyond language—certainly purged of Hecuba's histrionics, which it interrupts. With Andromache the play turns from exclamation (Hecuba) to narrative. There are many ways to do that speech; the only way you could ruin it would be through vulgarity or overstatement. Conversely, Hecuba's presence and speeches, with the equivalent of "ah"s and "woe is me"s, present brutal difficulties from both a dramatic and rhetorical perspective, and we have taken measures where necessary. As static moments and rhetorical clots, which might have their own resonance and inevitability in the ancient Greek, presented themselves, Katharine and I did everything we could think of to make them have an impact for readers of today and readers "north of the future." Our translation benefited enormously from David Slavitt's critical eye and skillful hand. His contribution far surpassed the efforts of even the most conscientious series editor, and we are deeply indebted to him.

Another testimony to the universality of the play's themes is a fantastic production staged by André Serban at Café La Mama. That production broke down the barriers between the seats and the stage, the audience and the actors. Serban's *The Trojan Women* was in neither English nor Greek, but a sort of composite language with a Greekish sound. The sounds of grief intensified; the women howled.

Translators' difficulties are legion and are among the most interesting of conundrums to puzzle within the boundaries of literature. Consider:

> Count no man happy until he is dead.

> *Mēdena nomizet' eutukhein prin an thanē(i).*

The language lends itself conveniently to this construction. Keep in mind that there are no pronouns in the Greek (which doesn't need pronouns because the verbs have personal endings). And the line has been reverberating through Greek poetry and drama for centuries. By the twentieth century it was renewed again by Yeats:

> Call no man fortunate that is not dead.
> The dead are free from pain.

The novelist Malcolm Lowry, in his cups, loved to exclaim, "Better to have never been born." Robert Lowell found another way to use the phrase in one of his best early poems, "Between the Porch and the Altar":

I quarreled with you, but am happy now,
To while away my life for your unrest
Of terror. Never to have lived is best.

We can surmise that in this play of all plays at a dramatic moment whose most distinctive feature is that it is populated by women, women who are both the subject and the subjected. This is not the time to have this phrase: this *sententia* refers to the oppressors who are presently drawing lots for the women. And since the Trojan men are dead, what are the Greek heroes doing? Drawing lots to see who will possess whom as a slave.

The task of translation here was, without changing the meaning of the Greek, at the very least, to keep the line in Hecuba's own frame: "Count no one happy until dead." Our earlier versions read, "Count no one happy until he's dead," and then, in an attempt to solve this problem of the speaker's gender, "Count no one happy until they're dead." The latter clearly didn't fly, and the former allowed for the deletion we arrived at. If the line risks awkwardness, the out-of-whack quality makes you notice the fact that they are all women. The reader may not be surprised now to hear that the line is already famous when Sophocles, echoing Aeschylus, uses it. By the time Euripides has it, he has his hat off to both of them.

This play is long familiar to English readers as *The Trojan Women*. We used *Daughters of Troy* because it reflects the idea of woman in an undefended city and that title most powerfully conveys a Euripidean sense of irony.

Mark Rudman

Cast

POSEIDON, god of the sea

ATHENA, goddess of wisdom

HECUBA, wife of Priam, mother of Cassandra and Polyxena

CHORUS of captive Trojan women

TALTHYBIUS, herald

CASSANDRA, daughter of Hecuba and Priam

ANDROMACHE, wife of Hector king of Troy, mother of
    Astyanax

MENELAUS, king of Sparta

HELEN, wife of Menelaus, taken by Paris to Troy

NONSPEAKING
    Astyanax, son of Hector and Andromache
    Greek soldiers
    Serving woman

*(The Greek camp before Troy, which has been sacked. Poseidon is
revealed on a platform, above the stage.)*

POSEIDON
    You see me here. Poseidon.
    On this last beach, risen from the bitter Aegean,
    where sea-girls trace arabesques on the ocean's floor.
    Far-sighted, I bound the land with waves,
    and with the clairvoyant god, Apollo,
    set up straight plumb-lines, piled
    stones into walls and towers.
    Troy had a special place in my heart.
    Troy is done for.
    Nothing will rise from this scattering of charred stones.   10
(pause)
    That lethal lady of the spear, Athena,
    got the cunning carpenter

from the town below the holy mountain
to construct a horse
quick with spearsmen in its hollow belly
and sent it through the gates: a deathtrap.
Not art, but artillery, the horse hurtles
toward the future with its forest of spears.
The sacred groves are empty.
Blood spills from the temple stairs   20
where Priam—as Zeus settled accounts—
was cut down before the ancestral altar.
The gold of Troy, the shields of the fallen,
stuff the holds of the victors' ships.
They wait for the rising levanter
to carry them home before seed-time.
The looters have had their day.
Two queens took my castle in Phrygia,
an unlikely pair, Hera and Athena, conniving together.
(pause)
Time to go. There's nothing for me here.   30
The gods are deserted: the altars are bare.
On these desolate shores, no one is left to honor us.
Troy is burnt to bitter ashes now.
Yesterday the Scamander ran with blood;
today, it is flooded with women's tears.
They are the prizes in a lottery:
Greek masters will divide the spoils:
this one for the south, that for the north,
these for Athens and Theseus' brood.
(long pause)
These that still wait in their tents   40
have not been spoken for.
Winnowed out, reserved for the high command,
Helen is among them, Leda's daughter,
who followed the spear that now prods her shapely back.
(pause)

And for Hecuba, that sack of bone and cloth,
sprawled before the city gates, tear-flooded?
She has reason enough to cry
even without knowing Polyxena is dead;
no one saw the butchering by torchlight
at Achilles' mound of that girl—her youngest daughter.   50
Priam's luck ran out: fifty children gone.
Aeneas is on his way to Rome.
Cassandra was untouched.
Apollo drove her half-mad and sent her
sunstruck into frantic divination.
But burly Agamemnon has hauled her to his dark bed . . .
So much for the short tragical history of the house of Troy.
Talk is cheap.

(pause)

Goodbye, then, my twilight capital,
your shining towers shimmered in their fall.   60
Your once blessed turrets that climbed the sky
would still be there
had she not brought you down.
Athena. Who has come to survey her work.

(He turns around. Athena has joined him on the platform.)

ATHENA

Great sir, I fear to approach you,
though the same stuff flows in our veins.
Grant me an interview. Our war is over.

POSEIDON

If you say so. What binds the gods
outlives these mortal quarrels.

ATHENA

We speak the same language, you and I.   70
And what I've got to say concerns us both.

POSEIDON
>Who deputized you to come here?
>Your father or some underling?

ATHENA
>No one sent me.
>I came on behalf of Troy,
>on whose battlements we pace.
>Now call forth your wind and water.

POSEIDON
>Now what? Did your hatred for Troy
>turn to a passion for its embers?

ATHENA
>Can I count on an angry ocean
>to advance our common cause?

80

POSEIDON
>Of course. But tell me, mercurial one,
>whose side you're on this time.

ATHENA
>I want the Trojans to exult for once.
>And a sea change for the Achaean fleet.

POSEIDON
>With what caprice you bound from love to hate,
>loving those you love too well,
>too much hating those you hate.

ATHENA
>They went too far.
>They desecrated my shrines.

90

POSEIDON

> I saw it, Ajax manhandling Cassandra.

ATHENA

> The Achaeans saw it, too,
> and made no move to stop it.

POSEIDON

> Your protégés, my dear. You let them loose on Troy.

ATHENA

> That was yesterday. Today,
> I seek their ruin with help from you.

POSEIDON

> Your will be done.
> What exactly do you have in mind?

ATHENA

> A homecoming—in which fish share their beds.

POSEIDON

> When? Where? Soon? Now?   100

ATHENA

> When they have pushed off from Ilium, and are sailing home,
> Zeus will blind them with rain, slam them with hail
> and unforgiving winds; he will blacken the noon.
> Zeus said he would lend lightning to scorch the Achaean ships,
> and blast the hulls, while you, Shipmaster,
> will turn the salt road into a whirlpool
> churning with foam and raise the great third wave,
> stormwrack the archipelago,
> and stuff the hollow of Cape Hell with corpses.
> After that, the Achaeans will know what's due us,   110
> when to honor our shrines, and when to bow.

POSEIDON
  Done.
(aside)
  So many words for one small favor.
(to Athena)
  I'll rouse the deep.
  Soon Myconos, the spiny reefs of Delos,
  Scyros, Lemnos, and the treacherous headlands of the north
  will be a graveyard for mariners.
  Go now to Olympus,
  borrow your Papa's lightning and wait
  for the Achaean fleet to set sail.   120
  The man's a fool who levels cities
  and makes a desert of holy ground,
  never knowing—his turn can be next.
*(The gods leave the platform. Hecuba, who has been crouching in the
                        shadows, now rises.)*

HECUBA
  Up Hecuba, you are not
  the darling of the gods after all,
  but you still can stand straight.
  Troy is no longer Troy,
  and I am queen of crones.
  Dust and ash sting my eyes.
  Our kingdom is come: to ruin.   130
(pause)
  The sea can swallow us.
  I brace myself against the changing of the gods.
  We near the narrows.
  We have no say in what course the helmsman takes;
  his face is covered. Was he ever our friend?

  I warn you.
  When too many hands grapple for the helm
  the odds are that you will never reach home.

I try to keep from crying for their return:
Troy, my children, the old king.   140
That wreck of a city is a burial mound now,
and we cower together here, moaning in grief.

Silence? Why? What does it gain Hecuba
not to speak? Why not
burst into the customary dirge
and groan, as though hell held me on its rack.
It is not right for a king's daughter to lie on the ground.

O head, O eyes, O brow,
O cage of words.
I wish I could give in to the roll of the waves,   150
submit, sway, and rake my cheeks
on the dark hull's barnacles
where the flow of the waves is of salt tears.
Give me a muse for broken lives,
a monody for wretchedness and disaster.
There are no dance steps for this song.
(pause)
Long ago, prows, oars,
a great fleet cut its way toward Ilium
on purple glass.
Skirting her harbors,   160
one day she made landfall.
I heard the fearful music
of flutes and men
before they stormed the beach.
They were working the cables
braided in Egypt
where they worship the dead
and know the underworld.

Gods!
They came to track down   170

that woman, Menelaus' slut,
skulking with her lover
behind the city's skirts.
She's no good, a disgrace to her twin
and the marsh where she was born.
On her account was Priam's throat slit—
a plowman in his prime, father of fifty sons . . .
Now dirge-driven Hecuba
is beached on ruin's strand.
Who's Hecuba?   180
Look at me.
I crouch outside Agamemnon's tent,
wrenched from home, a slave,
an old woman in mourning, broken,
my skull shaved, a clout upon my head,
where late the diadem stood,
and for a robe, a blanket,
fallen low in my city's fall.

Slower now . . .
O warriors' wives,   190
whose bronze swords green in the victors' holds.
Fresh brides to the dead,
look how Troy smolders.
(*Chorus walks out of the shadows.*)
No sound but a scream.
And I, like a mother, will raise
a clamor from the nest,
the plainsong for dark times;
I will sing, but not as I used to do:
"With Priam's scepter beating time,
girls and women in Phrygian rhyme,   200
the measure held, the music sweet,
the ground rejoiced with dancing feet."
Then the gods were near.

But I, a plain man in the ranks,   560
would never have wanted this woman's bed.
And you, you've lost your wits . . .
I fling your insults to Greece and praises of Troy
to the billowing winds.
Now you must follow me down to the ships,
a prize for the general.
(turning to Hecuba)
        And you, whenever the son
of Laertes comes to fetch you,
go where you're told. You will become
the serving woman of a woman   570
renowned for decency—
so they say who pass through Troy.

CASSANDRA *(responding to Talthybius)*
        And he too is a clever slave.
(turning now to Talthybius)
        Where do these "heralds,"
these lackeys to tyrants and states,
loathed by all mortals,
get their majestic name,
if not from hell?

        Do you mean that my mother
will go to Odysseus' palace?   580
Is Apollo's prophecy wind?
His oracle revealed she would die here in Troy,
and that riddle of his words
foretold still more in a future
too grotesque to utter.

        Odysseus is ignorant of what
he must now undergo.
When he has added ten years to the years
he has spent toiling here and arrives home alone,

he will look back on this Trojan War   590
    as a golden age.
(breaks off again)
    He knows nothing of the narrow passage
    between two rocks, the cliff where Charybdis
    dwells, nor of the Cyclops
    who keeps to the mountains and eats raw flesh,
    nor of Circe, on the Ligurian coast,
    who reduces men to swine,
    nor ships wrecked in mid-sea,
    nor his men becoming Lotus Eaters,
    nor the sacred cattle of the sun   600
    whose bleeding flesh will one day cry out
    in a language to make his own flesh crawl . . .
(pauses, and smiles, imagining the rest of it)
    And, to shorten this odyssey,
    once he has escaped the sea's jaws,
    he will descend, alive, into Hades,
    and when he returns he will find more
    troubles at home than he could have imagined.
    But why throw more shafts to add to the wounds
    of his labors?
(to Talthybius)
                              Go now, be off.
    My bridegroom awaits me in Hades.   610
    Agamemnon, to match your vileness
    you will be offered a vile night burial,
    far from the light, you who fancy yourself
    the leader of the Achaeans and a man of great deeds.
    My body will be hurled into a deep ravine,
    naked for the beasts to tear
    and the rough winter torrents will wash it.
    There I, Apollo's priestess,
    will lie unburied beside my bridegroom's grave.
(Cassandra takes the strands of wool that have bound her hair and
                    throws them into the air.)

Fall from my head now,   620
emblems I wore to delight you, Apollo,
my god of ecstasy, my prophet,
gone are my festival days.
Go, I tear you from my body
and cast these strands to the winds
to carry them to you, my god, my oracle.

Where is the general's ship anchored?
Where must I go to board it?
You won't have to wait any longer
for a breeze to fill the sails   630
to bring me away from this land:
a single fury flying to avenge three deaths.
Rejoice for me.
(to Hecuba)
     Mother, save your tears; you have nothing to weep for.
(As Hecuba collapses, Cassandra turns to the walls of Troy.)
     Beloved land,
     brothers who lie underground,
     and father to whom we owe our lives,
     it will not be long before you greet me below.
     After I have sacked the house of the sons of Atreus
     under whose hands we were destroyed,   640
     I will come victorious to the land of the dead.
(Talthybius takes Cassandra away.)

CHORUS
     The pity of it. See how our mistress lies there,
     her face in the dirt. Someone take her hand
     and help the wretched old woman up . . .

HECUBA
     Leave me here where I am.
     It gives me no pleasure to rise.
     O my daughters . . .

Fallen, I will fall again,
agony without end.
You cloud-riding gods,   650
once I thought of you as allies
and still I call out when mortal fortune
turns to misfortune.
Some dignity still clings to prayer.

Can I still raise my spirits
singing of the days when I,
as queen, lived well,
in this my song of departure?
Yesterday's joy vexes today's sorrow.
From royalty we came,   660
into royalty married,
and out of this union
brought forth shining sons
whose qualities—not numbers—
made them amazing
above all the Trojans,
men no other woman
of Troy or Greece
or any barbarian
could boast of bearing.   670

These sons I saw cut down
by Greek spears and this hair
I cut at their graves,
and over Priam, who planted this crop in me,
I wept.
The news of his death was not
brought to me by messenger,
but with these, my own eyes,
I saw him slaughtered
at our palace altar.   680
I saw my city taken.

I saw the daughters I raised
for worthy marriages
wrested from my hands
for other men,
and there is no chance that we will ever
see each other again.

My dirge now turns to Hecuba—
the final chord to all I have endured.
In what should have been my great good time   690
I will be brought to Greece as chattel.

They will set me to tasks
my aching bones are loath to perform.
To attend their thresholds.
They will have Hecuba, mother of Hector,
grind meal for their meals;
I, who descended from the high bed of kings,
will lay my sore back and wrinkled flesh
on hard floors for the rest
of my remaining nights.   700
My torn flesh will be wrapped
in rags disgraceful to the body
of a woman who was once
happy and prosperous.

This is my misery.
This is my fate.
This is the havoc
that the marriage of
one single female
has wreaked on me.   710
Cassandra, child, whose ecstasy
brings her closer to the frenzy of the gods,
in our wreckage you have lost
your virgin knot; and you, Polyxena,

where, where can you be?
Of all my many sons and daughters
who can help me now?
(to the Chorus)
Why do you try to lift me up?
How can you hope to help?
Lead me away, I who once   720
stepped like a queen through Troy
but now creep like a slave;
lead me to my bed of straw
on the earth's hard surface,
with a rocky pillow for my head,
so that I can at long last fall
and die, emptied by my weeping
for kings and queens and princes.
Count no one happy until dead.

CHORUS

> *Strophe*

Sing for me, Muse, of Ilium,   730
muse of new anthems,
a dirge for the dead you must invent,
for now my song and cry
will reach out to Troy
and tell of how I was deceived
and then ensnared by what moved
on four wheels, like a wagon;
how I, once destroyed,
was taken at spear-point
when the Achaeans left   740
the horse, armed to the teeth within,
at the gates of the city,
while its cheek-piece of gold
rumbled like thunder
from earth to heaven.

The watchmen stationed
on the rock ramparts of Troy
shouted out, "Go, Trojans,
who are quit of your troubles,
take this sacred wooden statue   750
as a gift, take it
to the temple of Athena,
Kore, Troy's virgin goddess,
daughter of Zeus."

No one stayed in:
no young woman;
no old man.
Beguiled by their festive songs
they found their ruin,
they were overrun.   760

Antistrophe

Swarming the gates, the Trojan troops
reached the band of Argives
hidden in the horse of mountain pine;
they rushed out frenziedly to honor
the virgin goddess of immortal horses
with a gift—Troy's demise.
They bound plaited ropes around the horse
as if dragging a ship's black
hull on logs, and brought it
to its berth on the stone foundation   770
of the temple soon to run with blood
and flood Troy.

Deep into the night we worked
under hope's spell,
while pipes cut from desert nettle
pulsed out high-pitched airs,
and the marvelous girls
danced and chanted and leapt.

And under the clusters of stars
blazing in the night sky,   780
the black glint from the hearth fires
cast a dark radiance on sleep.

Epode

In the palace chambers
I danced and sang
to Artemis, Zeus' daughter,
who favors the mountain heights,
until a murderous shriek shuddered the city,
shivered the citadel,
shook the little children;
their hands trembled with fear   790
as they clutched their mother's robes.
And Ares, child of Athena's cunning,
rose up from the horse's womb.

Blood washed the altars
and the desolate beds of young widows,
and their hair, cut in mourning,
was plaited like a triumphal crown for Greece,
but a symbol of mourning for Phrygia,
rich in sons. We filled Troy
with the sounds of our grief.   800

(*A wagon comes into the orchestra, heaped with the spoils of war and
carrying Andromache, wearing black and her hair
close-cropped in sign of mourning. She is holding
Astyanax. While the chorus continues speaking,
Hecuba rises again to her feet.*)

CHORUS
   Hecuba, do you see this woman
   being carried on this foreign carriage?
   Andromache!

And on the rhythmic oarlike motion
of her breasts follows the son
of Hector, dear little Astyanax . . .
(to Andromache)
     Where, mourning woman,
     where are they taking you, seated beside
     the bronze weapons of Hector
     and all the booty of Phrygia they came to hunt,   810
     the loot Achilles' son will hang
     as a victory offering from Troy
     in the shrines of Phthia?

ANDROMACHE
     My Greek masters are leading me as booty.

HECUBA
     O gods! O gods—

ANDROMACHE
                    Why cry for me?

HECUBA
                              Ai, ai . . .

ANDROMACHE
     This dirge for the pain . . .

HECUBA
                    O Zeus!

ANDROMACHE
                              . . . for this disaster . . .

HECUBA
     My poor children . . .

ANDROMACHE

We were once your children

HECUBA

Gone is our good fortune, gone is Troy,

ANDROMACHE

poor woman,

HECUBA

and the high birth of my children

ANDROMACHE

gone.

HECUBA

Lament then my . . .

ANDROMACHE

evils,   820

HECUBA

and the heartbreaking fate

ANDROMACHE

of the city,

HECUBA

which now smolders.

ANDROMACHE

Come my husband, come to me.

HECUBA

You cry out to my son, poor woman.
He's in the underworld.

ANDROMACHE
>Come, protect your wife.

HECUBA
>And you, whose blood stains Achaean hands,
>first-born of the children I once bore to Priam,
>come, take me down to Hades, to sleep.

ANDROMACHE
>Lord of my children,   830
>Priam, my father,

HECUBA
>come, take me down to Hades, to sleep.

ANDROMACHE
>These are great longings.

HECUBA
>These are pains that reach beyond the human.

ANDROMACHE
>Hurt for our ruined city.

HECUBA
>Pain has been heaped upon pain.

ANDROMACHE
>The gods have hated Troy
>from the time when your child Paris
>escaped death and, for the sake of a hated marriage,
>destroyed the city's tallest tower.   840

>Now vultures fill the sky like a dark cloud
>as the dead are piled by Pallas' temple.
>She made Troy a city of slaves.

HECUBA
    O Troy, my lost country,

ANDROMACHE
                    I weep for you, abandoned.

HECUBA
    You see the downfall of my home

ANDROMACHE
                        where I bore my son.

HECUBA
    O my children,
    your mother stands like Troy
    emptied of her daughters.
    Shrill laments enfold the great dead we mourn for.
    Tears pour down for our houses.   850
    But the dead feel pain no longer.

CHORUS
    Dirges and tears
    console the troubled.

ANDROMACHE *(calling attention to herself, her son, and the wealth of Troy in the wagon)*
    O mother of the man whose spear
    meant death to the Greeks,
    mother of Hector,
    do you see how bad things are?

HECUBA
    I see the work of the gods: how they raise
    towers to heaven out of clouds
    and destroy the dreams   860
    that seem so real.

ANDROMACHE

 I am being led away with my child,
 a war-prize.
 High birth has gone under the yoke,
 like a dream turned nightmare.

HECUBA

 Slavery's a hard necessity.
 Just now they've torn
 Cassandra away from me.

ANDROMACHE

 Ai, ai. Why don't the gods intervene?
 Now another man—a second Ajax—   870
 has arrived to violate your daughter.
(after a moment's hesitation)
 But your sickness goes beyond that.

HECUBA

 And my grief's immeasurable . . .
 disasters contend for prominence.

ANDROMACHE

 Your daughter Polyxena is dead:
 she was slaughtered at Achilles' grave,
 an offering to a lifeless corpse.

HECUBA

 Polyxena, Polyxena!
 So this was the light thread running
 through Talthybius' dark riddle.   880
(pause)

ANDROMACHE

 I saw her body with my own eyes
 I got down from this wagon.

I covered her with robes
and mourned for her.

HECUBA

My child, young victim,
I cry out for your part
in their sacrilegious sacrifice.
You are dead, my child.
But how horribly you died.

ANDROMACHE

She died her own death; she met   890
a fate that is sweet compared to my life.

HECUBA

Child, to see the light of day
is to be alive.
Death is nothing. In life, one harbors hopes.

ANDROMACHE

Mother, who gave me life, hear now
an argument to warm your heart.
Cancel the walk from cradle to grave—
better to be dead than live in anguish.
For whoever has exhausted hope
is numb to further pain,   900
but whoever knows good fortune,
when he has fallen in misfortune,
is distraught with the memory
of lost happiness.
Polyxena . . . she no longer sees the light
and is severed from these evils by death.
But I, who aspired to be well-thought-of,
I, who enjoyed some good measure of success,
have met disaster.
In Hector's house I practiced   910

every virtue women have perfected.
First, I stayed at home,
suppressing all desire to leave,
for doing this can ruin a woman
in the eyes of others—leaving the house,
whether or not there is just cause for blame.
Endowed with good judgment,
I did not need the company of other women
for wisdom to rub off on me.
Women can gossip, but not behind my doors.   920
To my husband I offered
a quiet demeanor, a modest, respectful look.
And I knew when to have the upper hand
and when to yield.
But when the report of these virtues
reached the Achaean camp
they were prelude to my demise.
The moment I was taken captive,
Achilles' son put in his bid for me.
I will be a slave in the polluted   930
house of murderers. And if I thrust
Hector's dear head from me
and open my heart to my present husband,
I will seem to have betrayed
the dead man.
But if I loathe my new husband,
I will earn the hate of my masters.
They say one night is enough
to ease a woman's resistance to a man.
I spit upon the woman who gives in   940
and abandons her husband to love another.

Even animals, lacking language and intelligence,
find it hard to switch mates.
And in Hector I had a man
who was all I could wish for in a husband;

he was wise, agile, courageous,
well-born; he cherished us.
When you took me from my father's house
I was a virgin.
You were my first man.   950
But now you are nowhere,
and I am to be taken across the seas to Greece,
forced to wear a slave's collar!

(to Hecuba)

Tell me now, does not the pain
of Polyxena,
for whom you are mourning,
seem minuscule against my fate.

I no longer possess mortal man and woman's
greatest companion, hope, nor am I so
witless as to think that the future holds   960
anything of worth in store for me.
Yet dreams are sweet.

CHORUS

You have fallen
as far as I have.
Your lament has taught me
the strain of my own lament.

HECUBA

I have never set foot on a ship,
but from stories I have heard and paintings I have seen
I know what it is to sail,
know that when a storm does not threaten them   970
sailors perform their various tasks:
the helmsman will keep to the rudder,
another will begin to furl the sail,
others will bail water from the hull.
But when the open sea should froth and break over the sides,

the sailors' discipline fails and they surrender to the force
of the running waves.
This is my destiny. I too am overwhelmed,
as this god-sent wave crests and breaks over me,
I cannot speak, I cannot get hold of my voice.   980
(pauses and turns to Andromache)
My love, my daughter,
you must accept Hector's fate
and stop this flood of useless tears.
They can't save him now.
Submit to your new master, endear him to you,
this way you will gladden every Trojan heart
and those who care for you.

And should you raise this child of my child
to be a man, one day your sons will found
another Troy, and our city   990
will be a city again.
(Talthybius arrives.)
Now another stage of our story begins.
Whom do I see coming now?
It is that pious lackey of the Greeks.
What new decisions will he announce?

TALTHYBIUS *(keeping at a distance from Andromache)*
Wife of Hector, who was the best of all the Phrygians,
do not hate me for the news I now convey.
It is not my choice to bring you the messages
the Greeks and the sons of Atreus have agreed to send.

ANDROMACHE
Say what you have to say, having already   1000
struck the first notes of a grim tale.

TALTHYBIUS
It has been decreed that this child . . .
How can I say it?

ANDROMACHE
No! Don't tell us that he's going
to a different master than his mother!

TALTHYBIUS
No Greek will ever be . . . his master.

ANDROMACHE
Do they want him to remain
here among the ruins
as the last remnant of what Troy was?

TALTHYBIUS
I know no good way to say the hard words.   1010

ANDROMACHE
I respect a decent reserve—
unless your words prove vile.

TALTHYBIUS
Your son must die. They will kill him.
There. Now you know.

ANDROMACHE
Kill Astyanax? This word *kill* sickens me
even more than the word *marriage*.

TALTHYBIUS
Odysseus has carried the day in the Greek assembly . . .

ANDROMACHE
The mind cannot take
this bleak information in.
All that remains is noise.   1020

TALTHYBIUS
. . . saying "We should not let the son
of such a valiant warrior live."

ANDROMACHE
>I wish Odysseus would win an argument
>that would result in Telemachus' death.

TALTHYBIUS *(not responding to Andromache)*
>but that he "must be hurled down
>from Troy's own towers."

(turns to Andromache)
>Let it be. Do the wiser thing and accept it.
>Don't cling to the boy. Bear your pain with dignity.
>What else is left to you when your strength is gone,
>when you have no power?   1030
>There's no one anywhere to help you.
>Consider, since you've no choice, the situation:
>your city and your husband are gone,
>you are at the mercy of others
>who are quite capable of mounting an attack
>against a woman alone.
>That is why I advise you to submit.
>Abandon your love of battle.
>I urge you to do nothing that would bring hatred against you,
>or, even more, to hurl curses against the Achaeans.   1040
>For if you so much as utter a word to enrage the army
>your son will be left unburied—
>denied even the routine lament they would recite
>over his body. But if you keep silent,
>if you control yourself in your misfortune
>this boy's body will not lie unburied;
>and the Greeks might treat you less harshly.

ANDROMACHE
>O child, dearest to my heart,
>honored too much for your own good,
>you will die at the hands of enemies   1050
>and leave your mother to grieve alone.
>Your father's high birth, which proved
>the source of safety for others,

has been your undoing. Doomed
is the bed we shared. Doomed is the marriage
which I entered when I entered Hector's chamber
with no thought that I would bear a son fit for a . . .
Greek sacrifice—and not a son to rule rich Asia.

Child . . . why are you crying?
Can you sense your doom?   1060
Why are your hands reaching out to clutch
my robe as if to nestle under my wings
like a baby bird? Hector will not rise up
from underground, nor grasp his famous spear
to come to the rescue,
nor will Hector's kin, nor the Phrygians.
No: you shall hurtle from the heights;
a bitter fall will break your neck,
your soul will sunder from your body
and there will be none to mourn you.   1070
Oh last and dearest embrace for a mother.
Oh sweet breath of your skin!
This is what comes of all my efforts.
All my labors that wore me out
were for nothing. These breasts that nourished you
with hope are dry.
Now, hug and kiss your mother one last time.
Come, lean against the woman who gave you life.
Wrap your arms around me. A kiss . . .

(kisses him and releases him to the Greeks)

O you Greeks, you Greeks, you skillful barbarians,   1080
why kill my son, who never harmed you?
O daughter of Tyndareus—you are no daughter of Zeus!
I say that you were born of many fathers:
the seed of Avenger, the seed of Spite,
of Gore, of Death and of all the Malevolent Crop
the hard earth yields.
I will never say that you were born of Zeus,

you who were delivered as a scourge
to Greeks and the rest of the world.

Die! From those doomed and beautiful eyes   1090
you have brought shame and ruin
to the shining plains of Troy.
(to the Greeks of the delegation)
Go on—take him.
Throw him down—if this is what you must do.
Throw him from these parapets,
feast on his child's flesh.
The gods have turned against us, they have destroyed us,
and we are powerless to rescue my son from death.
Cover this broken body and drive me to the ships,
and the fine marriage that faces me   1100
now that my child is dead.
(Talthybius lifts the child out of the wagon; it leaves the orchestra
through the parados to the audience's left, carrying
Andromache off.)

CHORUS

Troy, Troy, you have lost multitudes
on account of one woman's lust.

TALTHYBIUS

Come, boy, leave your sorrowing mother's arms
and mount the topmost ring of the towers.
The vote has been cast: you must die.
(to his men)
Take him.
Whoever is numb to pity and is a better friend
than I to the shamelessness of our decision
should utter proclamations such as these.   1110

HECUBA

O child, O son of a sorrowful son,
they have taken your life for no reason,

as a prize of war snatched from your mother and me.
What will happen to me?
Doomed child, what can I do for you?
We give you these—blows to our heads and breasts.
Our only power is in these actings out.
I cry out for you. What evil does not
inhabit us? What more do we need
to drive us over the edge?   1120

CHORUS

Strophe A

O Telamon, king of Salamis,
the island lashed by waves,
rich in flowers for the bees,
where first you built your dwelling,
slanting against the sacred
citadel of Attica,
where first Athena revealed
the olive branch, silver and gray,
stemming toward heaven
to adorn glittering Athens.   1130

You went, you went
to Ilium, Ilium,
with the son of Alcmene, the archer,
to prove your mettle with him,
to empty Ilium.

Antistrophe A

Our city, our city.
Before Heracles left for Greece.
when, furious that the immortal
horses promised him were withheld,
he led the best men Greece could offer   1140
and rested the oar that breaks water on the open sea

at the Simois, running smooth and easy;
then bound his ships' prows to the beachhead
and took his bow in his steady hand
to strike down Laomedon,
and batter down the stone wall
cut straight and true by Apollo,
devastating Troy
with the dark red breath of fire.

This is the second time   1150
the bloody spear toppled the walls
and scattered the stones
over the plains of Troy.

   Strophe B

And so, page-boy and son of Laomedon,
you walk in your great pride in heaven
pouring nectar into golden cups
and you have the great honor
of keeping Zeus' drinking vessels full,
for nothing—
for the city, who is your mother, burns,   1160
and a wailing rises from the sea's edge,
like the cry of a bird, fearful for her young,
a wailing for warriors,
a wailing for children,
a wailing for mothers.

Now the clear pools where you once bathed
and the running tracks and playing fields
have vanished.
But you, Ganymede, you flourish
beside Zeus' throne, your face   1170
luminous and lovely in grace and ease,
while below, Greek spears bring
Priam's domain to dust.

Antistrophe B

Eros, Eros,
desire and love,
love and desire,
a god once blazed
in the chambers of Dardanus,
and the eyes of the goddesses in the upper air
shone on you.   1180
You lifted Troy's towers to heaven.
You bound gods and men.
This is not the place
to slander Zeus.

(looking up and east to the mounting sun)

The goddess of day that men cherish
cast a dark glance on earth,
when, mounted on white wings,
she saw the citadel shattered.
She took a husband of this land,
bore a child, bore him up   1190
in a golden chariot drawn
by horses from the star-dazzled night,
spawning great hopes
for his homeland.
But for the gods,
Troy holds no more love potions.

(Menelaus has entered the orchestra toward the end of Antistrophe B. He
comes with a guard detail from the Greek army.)

MENELAUS

Today, the sun blazes on high and I
will soon lay hands again on Helen.
Many hardships have I, Menelaus,
endured with the Achaean fleet.   1200
I came to Troy not as the multitude suppose—
for a woman—but to retaliate
against the guest who betrayed my hospitality

pirating Helen from my house.
He's paid his penalty, with the gods' help;
he and his kingdom have groveled under the Greek spear,
and I have come for the woman from Sparta—
my mouth will not form the word "wife"
to name her, who was once mine.
And I know that in these captive quarters   1210
she is numbered among the other daughters of Troy.
Those who bent their spears to win her
have surrendered her to Menelaus
to execute or, if I please, to reprieve
and bring back home to Argos.
It was my decision
to oppose her destined end in Troy,
to bring her aboard a ship
that ploughs the sea to Grecian shores
and hand her over TO BE KILLED THERE   1220
as requital for her kinsmen, dead in Ilium.

o his men)

Go, my attendants, to her shelter,
drag her by her hennaed hair,
and when the wind rises from the east
we will go with her to Greece.

ECUBA

O Zeus, you who are support for the earth,
and have your seat upon the earth,
whoever you are,
difficult to know, to grasp—
Zeus, whether nature's necessity or mortal intelligence,   1230
I call upon you.
Traveling upon a silent path
you direct all mortal things toward justice.

ENELAUS

What is this? You risk addressing the gods like this?

HECUBA

> You have my praise, Menelaus,
> if you intend to kill your wife,
> but be careful not to look on her again
> lest she ensnare you with desire;
> for she magnetizes men's eyes,
> destroys cities and sets the houses on fire within.   1240
> She's adept at the black arts.
> I know her, you know her,
> and so do those who have suffered on her behalf.

(Helen has been escorted from the tent. She is flanked by two Greek
soldiers who hold her arms. Helen is carefully
dressed and her hair meticulously plaited.)

HELEN

> Menelaus! Such treatment must be preface
> to some tale not fit for human ears.
> Rudely jostled, taken from the house,
> put on display by your attendants—
> I have no doubt that you hate me
> but still I wish to speak. I must know.
> Have the Greeks made up their minds?   1250
> Have you? Am I to live?

MENELAUS

> The entire army chose to put your death
> in the hands of the man you wronged.
> It wasn't a close decision.

HELEN

> Will I be allowed to respond
> to this judgment and argue?
> If I am to die, I am
> put to death unjustly.

MENELAUS

> I didn't come to discuss, woman, but to kill you.

HECUBA

    Hear her out, Menelaus, she must not   1260
    die without a hearing.
    But you will convict her after our argument.
    You know nothing of the horrors within Troy,
    and these, added to the sum of your complaints,
    will condemn her to death
    beyond any appeal.

MENELAUS

    This will take time. She may speak if she desires.
    But I grant this gift not as a favor to her, Hecuba,
    but for your sake—and to hear what she has to say.

HELEN

    If you've already condemned me as your enemy,   1270
    you will not absolve me no matter how well
    or how poorly I speak;
    we have tutors in rhetoric in Sparta, too.

    To start: First off, this woman, in giving
    birth to Paris, gave birth to this catastrophe.
    Second charge: the old man, Priam,
    destroyed both Troy and me when he failed
    to kill the infant, that bitter dream-image
    of a torch, then called—heroically—Alexander.
    Mark how the story unfolds from there.   1280
    This man had to judge a contest
    that joined three goddesses.
    Athena offered Alexander
    the Phrygian army, the destruction of Greece.
    Hera promised, if Paris chose her over
    the others, that he, an Asian,
    would be absolute master of all Europe.
    And Aphrodite, dazzled by my looks
    like everyone else, promised to give me to him
    should she surpass the other goddesses in beauty.   1290

Consider now this turning,
and don't forget, I was first prize.
Cypris is victorious over the other goddesses,
and this, then, is the great good my marriage did for Greece.
You are not under the power of the barbarian;
you came neither to be defeated in battle
nor to fall under tyranny.

The very source of Greece's fortune
caused my destruction—
beauty has been my undoing.   1300
Am I reviled by the very man from whose hands
I ought to have received a crown of thanks?

You will say that I have not yet spoken
to the most obvious charge of all—
that I stole away from your home in secret.
He came accompanied by a goddess . . .
no minor deity.
When he came to me, to this woman you see before you—
call him Alexander if you like or Paris—
he found me alone because you, you fool,   1310
had left me there in Argos
when you set sail for the Cretan shores.

Hear me out—this is just one point.
Everything I have yet to say concerns me, Helen.
Why in the world would I have gone
with this stranger, betrayed
my country and home
if I were in my right mind?
Treat the goddess as you are treating me
and become mightier than Zeus,   1320
who, for all his power over the other
gods and divinities,
is slave to that goddess.

Reason enough to forgive me!
From here, a more plausible account of my actions follows.
You will say that when Alexander
died and descended to the inner gorges of the earth,
I ought to have left my home in Troy—
being no longer compelled by a goddess to share his bed—
and gone down to the Argive ships.   1330
And this is exactly what I tried to do.
The gatekeepers and the sentinels
on the ramparts are my witnesses!
Time after time they caught me
in the act of trying to steal away, with ropes
hanging from the battlements to the ground.
But my new husband, Deiphobus,
pulled me away by force and kept me,
all without permission of the Phrygians.
How then, my husband, could I die   1340
a just and deserved death at your hands?
My marriage to one man was under compulsion:
my life in Troy—bitter servitude.
No victor's life.
If you want to be omnipotent, go ahead—
but it defeats your purposes to ask for my death.

CHORUS

Come, queen, defend
your children and your country,
dissolve this woman's
persuasive eloquence.   1350
She speaks well but has done ill:
a terrible gift.

HECUBA

To begin: I will be the ally of the goddesses
and prove that what this woman says is not just.
It is my opinion that Hera and the ice maiden

could never reach such a pitch of folly
as would entice Hera to sell Argos
to the barbarians or make snow-white Athens
slave to the towers of Troy.

These goddesses did not come to Ida in a spirit of   1360
playfulness and pride and pleasure in their beauty.
What could have made Hera, a goddess herself,
contract a sudden passion for beauty?
To claim a better husband than Zeus?
Or was Athena out to marry one of the gods?
It was she who in her disdain for marriage
asked for the gift of virginity from her father
and steered shy of men's beds.
Do not make fools of the gods   1370
to prettify your vice. Do not
think you will persuade the wise;
you're sure to fail.
Now you said "Cypris"—this part is truly absurd—
came with my son to Menelaus' house.
Could she not, Zeus-like, have brought
you and all of Amyclae to Ilium
without budging from heaven?
My son's beauty was aphrodisiac;
once you beheld him you couldn't vanquish   1380
the rampage of sexual thoughts
that flooded your mind.
For mortals all forms of folly
gather under Aphrodite's name.
But when she set eyes on my son,
decked in brilliant gold and Oriental garb,
Helen lost her reason.
(addressing Helen directly)
         At home you lived a Spartan life.
         But you hoped that once out of Sparta
         you would find in the capital of Phrygia

a city flowing with streams of gold,   1390
a sumptuous city to satisfy your dreams
of extravagance. Menelaus' palace
wasn't up to your standards—
too cramped for you and lacking in luxuries.

Enough of this. You claim my son
forced you to come here. Which Spartan
witnessed this? And what did you cry out?
Castor and his twin Pollux
were still in Sparta; they had not yet risen.

You came to Troy,   1400
the Argives dogging your tracks.
And there was a conflict
whenever you heard
that Menelaus had the advantage over Paris,
but you sang his praises, hoping to pain my son
with his great rival for your love.
But when the Trojans' luck was running,
Menelaus was dirt in your eyes.
This was your practice and you kept
your focus on fortune,   1410
looking to follow her ways, not virtue's.

Now to the next point: you claim you tried
to steal away by letting yourself
down from the battlements on plaited ropes
and that you stayed in Troy against your will.
Tell me then: who ever found you fastening
a noose or sharpening a sword—actions
a truly noble woman would take
out of longing for her former husband?
Often I had pleaded with you: 1420
"My daughter, get out of the city. My sons
can marry other women; I will escort

you back to the Achaean ships and help
you steal away. Put an end to this war
between us and the Greeks."
But you looked on this advice with bitterness.

Sullen and haughty in the house of Alexander,
you expected us Asians to kneel and cower.
This was your attitude—
but still unsatisfied you defied your widowhood,   1430
and, adorned in silks of many colors,
you looked upon the same azure
sky as your dead husband.
I could spit in your face. You!—
Who ought to have pretended humility
and worn mourning's tattered garments,
shuddering with fright, your hair cropped
close by a sharp Scythian knife.
You should have shown more modesty
than brazenness for past sins.   1440
(to Menelaus)
Wreathe Greece in victory, kill this woman,
prove worthy of yourself, and establish
this law as law for all other women:
whoever betrays her husband, dies.

CHORUS LEADER
Menelaus proves a worthy
descendant of Atreus.
Absolve yourself of the charge
of womanliness.

Be virile in the eyes of Greece,
prove yourself against your enemies.   1450

CHORUS
Menelaus, show your mettle.
Give your wife what she deserves.

MENELAUS

    Your argument concludes mine.
    This woman went of her own accord
    from my house to a stranger's bed.
    And invoked Cypris out of self-love only.
    So now she faces the soldiers, armed with stones,
    and pays, in an instant,
    for the long suffering of the Achaeans.

    Die, and learn,   1460
    never try to shame Menelaus.

HELEN

    Don't. Menelaus, I beg you, don't assign
    the madness and disease of the goddess
    to me and have me die. Forgive.

HECUBA

    Do not be a traitor
    to your fellow soldiers who died
    for this woman's face.
    I pray to you on their behalf
    and on behalf of their children.

MENELAUS

    Enough, old woman, she's nothing to me.   1470
    I will command my men to take her to the ships
    and away to Greece.

HECUBA

    Wait! Don't let her step foot on your ship.

MENELAUS *(laughing)*

    Why? Is there more of her than there used to be?

HECUBA

    No lover lives who can put
    the object of his love out of mind.

MENELAUS

That depends on the lover's mind.
You'll get what you ask for. It follows.
She shall not set foot on the ship I sail in.
And when she arrives in Argos she will die   1480
the death she deserves and be heaped with shame,
a lesson in restraint for all women.
It will not be an easy lesson,
but her doom will transform their lust to fear
even if it fuels their hatred.

(Menelaus, his men, and Helen exit stage left.)

CHORUS

Strophe A

It is a fearful thing to be flung
from the hand of the living god.
Zeus handed Troy's smoking altars to the Greeks:
the steamy mulch poured on the flame,
the myrrh that climbed the azure roof,   1490
the tall citadel and Ida's high ridges
thick with ivy, cut with snow-fed culverts,
mountaintop the sun strikes first and last—
once filled with light, once sacred.

Antistrophe A

Gone are the offerings and the holy cries
of the dance in the dark night
and the night-long festivals,
the golden statues of the gods;
and the moon-dials that number and trace
the moon's phases in the nights' supernal silence,   1500
that number the months.
What did you feel
in the blaze of the besieged city
as the flames licked your chair?

Did the smoke get in your eyes? Make you blind?
Was Troy the sacrifice you had in mind?

Strophe B

O young men, O my mate,
O you dead, now spirits stumbling
on the wrong shore,
while your bodies lie   1510
above ground, mud-caked and rotting,
for ravens to prey on.
You gods—build me a sea-going vessel
with darting wings
to bring me to the pastures of Argos,
where horses graze,
where Cyclopian walls
break the sky.
They are herding the children
like heifers, lowing, down to the gate.   1520
(Chorus turns to Hecuba.)
MA—MA—
The herdsmen of Achaea are taking me out
of your sight, away from your arms
leading me down to the midnight boats
whose oars clip the waves
all the way to port
hard by the double-gated island,
Pelops' keep,
where fathers eat their children.

Antistrophe B

Let that thunder   1530
break the toy ship in the middle sea,
clap the oar with fire,
break Menelaus.
He exiled me, enslaved me,
a wife to constant sorrow.

Break the mirrors, girls' toys,
Helen's first love,
 would that they were all shattered.

Menelaus—may he never return
to Laconia, to the limestone cliffs   1540
of that grubby backwater
where men live like stones;
to his father's smoky hearth,
to the bronze fault of the goddess.
Who looked on
when he forced great Hellas
to a filthy union
made in the mud of the river bed?

Exodos

*(The chorus has caught sight of Talthybius and a detail of Greeks who
         have appeared with the body of Astyanax.)*

Disaster wears many masks
on the face of the earth.   1550
Look now, powerless wives of Trojan men,
at the body of Astyanax here before us.
The Danaans hurled him, a grim missile,
from the battlements, and now bear his corpse.

TALTHYBIUS

Hecuba, there is a last ship
with oars poised to sweep the sea—
send the booty won by Achilles' son
to the fog-bound coast;
his oars are already dipped in the water;
primed by news of new troubles for the old man.   1560
Necessity's face had driven him from his land,
urged him to leave sooner than he would have liked,
accompanied by Andromache,

and my eyes filled with tears,
as they cast off—
she, calling for her lost country,
addressing Hector's tomb.
And she asked him
to lay this body in the earth;
this child of your Hector 1570
fell from the walls, the breath broken from his body.
This terror to rout the Achaeans,
this bronze-backed shield,
which this boy's father kept at his side,
she asked him not to bring it home
or to the same chamber where she would marry.
The mother of this dead child
did not want to look on this spur to grief
and sorrow, and instead of a cedar coffin
and an enclosure of stone, 1580
she asked him to bury her child in Hector's shield.
(*Talthybius indicates Hector's shield.*)
She asked that he be delivered to your arms
so that you can wrap his body
in a robe and garland his head
with whatever remains to you.
For she is gone; her lord's haste has kept her
from giving her child rites of the grave.
Once you have dressed the body in death's garments,
and we have piled earth over him,
we'll set sail. 1590
Let us move on.
I have spared you one part of this labor.
Fording the water of the Scamander
I washed his body, I washed the blood from his wounds.

Now I am going to break the earth and dig his grave
and hope that my labors and yours will soon
become one as our ship begins the long voyage home.

HECUBA

You men, put the round-rimmed shield of Hector
back on the ground.
It pains my eyes to gaze on it.   1600
You Greeks, whose heavy spears outweigh your brains!
What did you fear in this child?
Why create new forms of slaughter?
Did you cower out of fear
that he would resurrect Troy?
Even when good fortune favored
Hector and his many men,
there was still blood shed on our side.
And you were cowards even then.
But now, when our city has been taken   1610
and the people slain,
you were frightened of a baby as small as this?
I have no patience with anyone
who does not temper impulse with reason.

O my dear child, what a dingy way to go.
Had you died a man, armor clanging
as you fought to save your city,
a husband come to kingship,
which puts gods and men on the same plane,
you would have been blessed—   1620
if anything on earth is blessed.
But you have only witnessed these blessings,
and recognized what they are
without knowing them; you never had time
to enjoy, my prince, what was rightfully yours.

Unhappy child, how cruelly have these great walls
your fathers built so high, these towers of Apollo,
stripped the hair from your head
your mother combed and kissed so often.

Now gore grins from its broken bones—   1630
the rest sickens speech.
O small hands, how sweet
your likeness to a father's hands!
Now you lie before me limp and broken.
And dear mouth, now silent,
many were the brave words you uttered.
Child, you deceived me.
Scampering to my bed, you'd cry out,
"Grandma, make sure when you die
that I will cut a big lock of hair from my head,   1640
and come to your grave.
I and my friends will feast at your funeral
and whisper sweet prayers."

(pause)

It is not you, prince, who will bury me;
I bury you in your youth.
I, an old woman, dispossessed
of my city and my relations,
now must I lay your battered body
in the ground.

All our affection and embraces,   1650
all the care I lavished on you,
those long nights, those sleeps of the past,
when you slept in my palace
are gone.
What fitting epitaph could a poet
fashion for your gravestone?
"A SMALL BOY'S BODY LIES HERE,
WHOM THE GREEKS KILLED, OUT OF FEAR."
A rhyme incised in stone to scorn those Greeks.
But, even denied your inheritance,   1660
you will carry
Hector's bronze-backed shield
to the grave.

Shield, shield that once
guarded Hector's strong arm,
you have lost your guard and protector.
How sweet the deep impression
that lies in its hollow and the sweat
of the grip in its rounded rim
that Hector often lifted   1670
to his chin in the hard press
of battle to wipe his brow.
(She hands a gold-embroidered robe to her serving woman.)
Come, throw this garment over him.
It is all we can offer.
Our fate and the dark god behind it
does not grant us beauty.
(to Astyanax)
Take it, from what I have to give.

CHORUS

That mortal is a fool who,
heady with brief success,
rejoices for steady prosperity.   1680
Our luck, good or bad,
reels like a lunatic,
lurching left and right.
Our mortal lot's haphazard;
no happiness comes to us
without the will of the gods.
Yes, these women are bearing
some spoil of war, a garment, to adorn his body.

HECUBA

O child, your father's mother places this
victor's garment of lost wealth over you.   1690
You have won no victory in the horse race
or in archery, contests so valued by the Phrygians,

but not to excess.
Helen, whom the gods loathe,
has forever wrested away these joys,
taken your life, destroyed your home.

CHORUS

    Your words tear
    at me; my heart
    goes out to Astyanax,
    once lord of my city.   1700

HECUBA

    I now wrap your body in the fine
    embroidered garments of the East
    and cover it.
    You would have worn these robes at your wedding
    to an Asian princess . . .
(She places Astyanax's body in the hollow of Hector's shield, and
addresses the shield.)
    And you, mother of victories,
    once held high in triumph,
    shield that was once part of Hector,
    I place this crown upon you.
    You will not die—if you die with this body.   1710
    It is better far to honor you
    than to honor words,
    the arms of Odysseus,
    that sophist and scheming coward.

       Antiphonal Lament

CHORUS

    Ai, . . . Ai!
    The earth will swallow you, child,
    as grief's bitter seed.
    Mother, lament.

HECUBA
>Daughters, lament

CHORUS
>A cry for the dead—Hecuba.

HECUBA
>A cry for the dead

CHORUS
>This is the cry I utter,
>for your grief will never be erased.

HECUBA
>I shall heal your wounds with these wrappings,
>*(covers his head in winding cloth)*
>>I who in my grief bear the physician's name
>>but not his balm.
>>Your father will look out for the rest;
>>in the underworld.

CHORUS
>Strike. Strike the head.
>Rain blows down. Fist on fist

HECUBA
>Women, who are . . . most dear to me . . .

CHORUS
>Hecuba, what will you tell your daughters?

HECUBA *(after a silence)*
>So. The gods cared not a whit.
>They made sure I would suffer
>and that Troy be detested
>above all other cities.
>Our sacrificial smoke never reached heaven.

But if a god had not turned our world upside down
and buried these towers under the earth,
we would have been ciphers   1740
and our music unsung
by bards north of the future.

Go, bury this body in the trench.
He is adorned enough—for a dead boy.
Honors are like detritus to the dead.
The corpse receives heaped offerings at the grave.
The living crave these hollow displays.

Second Antiphonal Movement

CHORUS
    Luckless woman, Andromache's great hopes
    for you are dashed and you who were
    blessed by your birth are now cursed   1750
    by the brute fact of your death
(looking up to the walls of Troy on the stage before them)
    What do I see? What hands are these
    with torches darting here and there
    on Ilium's fiery crest?
    Some grim new catastrophe
    appends Troy's story.

TALTHYBIUS *(to his troops)*
    I address myself
    to you, captains, who are under orders
    to raze Priam's city,
    do not hoard the bright fire in your hands   1760
    but hurl your torches into Troy
    so that we can depart triumphant,
    having leveled Ilium.
(to the Trojan captives)
    And you, daughters of Troy,
    to give two shapes to one and the same command,

haste your way to the Achaean ships
when the generals signal the trumpets
to blast to high heaven
and carry you away from these shores.
(to Hecuba)
And you, old woman, steeped in suffering,   1770
follow these men whom Odysseus has sent for you;
you fell to him in the distribution of the spoils.
Your lot will follow you from this land.

HECUBA *(wails)*
I have now reached
the frontier of my suffering.
Grief can go no further.
I leave the country with my city in flames.
(turns to the city)
Come, old bones, make one good last effort
that I may greet my ailing city,
city that once exhaled that greatness and pride   1780
to which humankind aspired
among barbarian nations.
Troy, your renown will be stripped from you.
They are feeding you to the fire,
and leading us away from the land
and into slavery.
(pause)
Gods!
But why should I call upon the gods now?
They haven't answered.
(addresses herself)
Hecuba—run to the pyre.   1790
The crowning act is to die
in my city's conflagration.

TALTHYBIUS
Unhappy woman, it's the gods of your own torment
Who've overcome you.
(to Odysseus' men)

Take her away.
Don't hesitate. She must be taken as a symbol
of this conquest and delivered to Odysseus.

Strophe A

HECUBA
    Son of Cronus, Phrygian,
    counselor, begetter, father,
    do you witness our suffering?   1800

CHORUS
    He has witnessed it.
    But the mighty city
    is a city no more.
    All that remains
    of Troy is a name.

Antistrophe A

HECUBA *(wails)*
    Ilium glitters.
    The citadel blazes, the buildings,
    the high temples and palisades, all burn.

CHORUS
    Our land, fallen in warfare,
    vanishes like a bird lifting on wings of smoke   1810
    to the edge of vision.
    Fire rages through hungry halls,
    swept on by torches.

Strophe B

HECUBA
    Land, earth, from you my children grew.

CHORUS
    Troy.

HECUBA *(beating upon the earth)*
O my children, listen, know your mother's voice.

CHORUS
Is that shrill wail to invoke the dead?

HECUBA
Yes, I place my old limbs on the earth
and strike the ground with both my fists.

CHORUS
We too fall to our knees   1820
and call upon our dead husbands
underground.

HECUBA
Hear us, they lead us away, as booty.

CHORUS
Sorrow is your song.

HECUBA
They bear us to a slave's quarters

CHORUS
from our homeland.

HECUBA
Priam, Priam dead,
without a grave,
without a friend, without kin,
without inkling of what   1830
I suffer now.

CHORUS
Black death clouded his eyes,
holy death, unholy slaughter.

Antistrophe B

IECUBA

Great houses of the gods, dear city,

CHORUS

                                                dear city.

IECUBA

All you have now is bloody flame
and the tip of a spear.

CHORUS

Soon you will collapse nameless to the ground.

IECUBA

And the cloud of dust and ash will lift on wings of smoke
toward bright heaven and blind me to my home.

CHORUS

The name of this land plunges into black night.   1840
Loss rushes upon loss.
Troy destroyed is Troy no more.

(A deep rumble is heard.)

IECUBA

Did you hear, did you hear that?

CHORUS

Our citadel has given way.

IECUBA

Destruction's quake

CHORUS

                                        overwhelms our city

(Odysseus' men lift her from the ground and lead her from the stage left;
the other women are herded out as well.)

HECUBA
>   Tremble. Still, walk away.
>   Get going, old bones
>   down to the dawn of slavery.

CHORUS
>   O Troy, farewell.
>   The Achaean ships   1850
>   attend our going.
>   We must move on.
> *(Exeunt.)*

The Phoenician Women

translated by
Richard Elman

Translator's Preface

Even in the stilted antimacassar prose and verses of the Loeb Classical Library's literal translation of Euripides' play, there exist sharp dramatic conflicts. *The Phoenician Women* is a play of force, a series of confrontations—Jocasta with impulsive Polynices, Polynices with Eteocles, Creon with Antigone and with his disgraced brother-in-law, the blind king Oedipus—and all these are played out against the massing armies of Argonauts and Thebans on both sides of the walls of the old seven-gated city in the midst of a continuing crisis over succession.

For beleaguered Thebes, the purgation of the descendants of Laius who have been perverted by defiance of the Oracle does not necessarily have to come about in the way it does. In the course of this powerful play nearly all the principal characters suffer unexpected catastrophes: the sons of Oedipus kill each other; Jocasta slays herself; the son of Creon sacrifices himself misguidedly so Thebes may survive. Only the former king, Oedipus, is legally banished forever from the city, accompanied by his willful daughter, Antigone.

In preparing my adaptation of this text for a contemporary reader in English, I wanted to keep the sharp confrontational outlines of the play and to make the language clear, available, and vivid. This, then, is ancient Greek drama with some urban twentieth-century American candor. I've tried very hard to avoid overblown rhetoric and the jingle-jangle-jingle of doggerel, but also the hip demotic English of one who grew up digging the jive tragedies of Charlie Parker and Billie Holiday.

Of my experience as adapter, at this point I confess to finding myself in agreement with disenfranchised Polynices, who remarks in a soliloquy early on:

> To those who risk all,
> all seems so perilous just as soon as they
> find themselves on hostile ground . . . (306 – 8)

I am a novelist and poet; being on the "hostile ground" of classical literature in translation, I've trusted David Slavitt and others as Polynices did h mother. They have read the manuscript-in-progress a few pages at a tim and thus sustained me in completing the task. But it's also true that from th first I felt myself given over to Euripides, this most capable of writers, wh made his drama so sharp with interpersonal conflicts and frustrating reso lutions that I could easily find it in me to trust the cleanly outlined writing

Euripides is said to be the most contemporary of the Greek dramatist and it's easy to see why. His characters take issue with each other in ver human ways, face to face, with little intervention of other powers. Readin this play we feel we are in the presence of a recognizable family pitte against one another. It's a drama in which the guilt-ridden mother, Jocast even now reaches out to her sons to conciliate them, though she still unable to accept herself for cohabiting with Oedipus, her own son, and t forgive the blinded former king for his sinful embraces.

It's as though Euripides were to remind Attic audiences that in every cri sis, such as the one that comes on here after the abdication of Oedipu opposing positions harden, making compromise difficult. Though the god bestow certain undeniable ways and conditions on humans, it's our huma task to live honorably within such arrangements. If we are not prepared t compromise, the writer advises us, we must surely be prepared to die.

Eteocles was by agreement bound to share the throne of Thebes with hi younger brother Polynices. His failure to abide by this succession agree ment brought about the sequence of actions that led to his own undoing i hand-to-hand combat with his brother before the gates of Thebes, and t his brother's death, as well, in that same place. Euripides is always present ing his characters with choices, and if they fail to choose in their ow best interests—as their mother reminds them—they bring destruction o themselves and others. I suppose this is why he is said to be an "ethical dramatist. His ethical choices are operational in the dramas, not distinct an apart, and to act out of senseless meanness leads to the absurd end of deat invariably a form of blind self-murder. Eteocles could try to be conciliatory but he is greedy. He tells his mother:

> I'd climb up to the stars or to the sun,
> or plunge beneath the earth, if I could,
> to maintain power here . . .   (540–42)

The chorus in *The Phoenician Women* reminds us again and again of the heroic acts of the characters' forebears, whether mortal or divine. It evokes heroic past in contrast to this peevish and stubborn quarrel between brothers. It was not impossible to dramatize this family squabble in conflicting passages with irony and care, but I sometimes found the choruses more of a challenge. When the portent of some of the mythological parallels was obscure to me, I omitted them: a line here, a paragraph there. There seemed to be more than enough clan mythologizing to bear these slight excisions.

This quarrel within this Theban royal family over succession is a somewhat larger-than-life representation of what goes on in too many families about preferment and the rivalry of siblings. It took place in my own family when I was growing up. Vexed with envy, I called my older brother "stinky Leonard!"; Polynices taunts Eteocles as "cowardly."

The quarrel between Creon and Antigone about burying Polynices is also an assertion by Antigone of counter-generational values. She knows the laws of Thebes as well as her uncle does, but refuses to dishonor her brother as a traitor with her uncle's tedious legalisms. As a caring mother, Jocasta advises Polynices to "narrow" his thoughts to the matter at hand and leave out "old arguments." She counsels Eteocles to appreciate that "Nature gave all men the law of equal rights." Though she seems persuasive, she cannot move her son to forgo enmity. They are locked by rage in their positions, counterpoised to each other until they fight and harm each other, and, too late, forgive.

There's very little excess of action or verbiage in this drama. It is stark and argumentative, a standoff that can only lead to disaster. The only pathos is in the final exit from Thebes of Oedipus accompanied by Antigone. However, as even she makes clear, her father's fate was of his own making. He is the most unhappy of mortals, and it's his own fault. She departs from Thebes with him out of loyalty, though not without loathing and disgust.

When Antigone tells her father that he has brought about his own degradation, we recognize Euripides as our contemporary. We are always of two minds about these royal characters. Seeing the justice of their positions, we also see the careless self-indulgence of their arguments. This back-and-forth between Eteocles and his brother Polynices may be the painful dramatization of our own two minds.

Cast

JOCASTA, wife of Laius, wife and mother of Oedipus, former
   queen of Thebes
ANTIGONE, daughter of Jocasta
OLD SERVANT
CHORUS OF PHOENICIAN WOMEN
POLYNICES, son of Oedipus and Jocasta
ETEOCLES, present king of Thebes and son of Oedipus and
   Jocasta
CREON, brother of Jocasta and adviser to Eteocles
TIRESIAS, a soothsayer
MENOECEUS, father of Creon and Jocasta
MESSENGER
OEDIPUS, dishonored former king of Thebes
NONSPEAKING
   Daughter of Tiresias
   Attendants

(Jocasta stands in front of the royal palace at Thebes.)

JOCASTA
   Cruel sun, blazing through heaven
   on a golden chariot, spewing fire,
   what evil curses you have hurled
   on Thebes from the day that Cadmus,
   fleeing Phoenicia's coastline,
   arrived in this kingdom? He took Harmonia
   to be his wife, Cypris' daughter,
   and sired Polydorus, father of Labdacus,
   from whom came Laius.
(pause)
   My father, Menoeceus, named me Jocasta;   10
   Creon is my brother. I married Laius.

After many years together, when my womb remained barren,
my mate appealed to Apollo that he grant us
male heirs to our throne, but the god replied:

"Lord of Thebes, famous for horses,
do not sow your seed against
the will of the gods. If you have a son,
in manhood he will murder you, and
all your household will wade in pools of blood."

One night my lord was drunk and   20
took me and begot a son, and after,
frightened by his act, remembering Apollo's
warning, he handed the infant I had borne
to the rough hands of shepherds
to expose on steep Cithaeron.
With iron spikes he pierced our baby's
ankles. Thus his name, Lame-Foot. In Greek:
Oedipus. That child survived, and
Polybus' horsemen found him and took him
home to their mistress to be nursed.   30
Pretending to her husband she was its mother,
she nursed Oedipus, but when he grew to manhood
he guessed, or someone told him, and he set forth
to Phoebus' shrine to ask who his parents really were.

And Laius, my husband, seeking even then
to confirm that the child cast out was dead,
encountered Oedipus at a fork in the road at Phocis.
In the summer dust father and son held their ground.
"Stand away and let a prince pass by,"
my lord's charioteer ordered Oedipus,   40
who did not obey. When the rushing steeds
of Laius scraped his ankles bloody,
in pain and rage my son slew his royal father
and returned to Polybus with the chariot booty.
Later on my brother Creon proclaimed

whoever could decipher the riddle of the Sphinx
ravaging Thebes at the death of my lord
would have me in marriage as his reward.
Strangely, only Oedipus, my unknowing son,
could understand her three-legged riddle.   50
He became my second lord and sovereign of this land,
defiling his mother's body to rule in Thebes—
wretch—as unwitting as I, who was given to him
as prize and produced from his bed
two more sons in lustful ease, Eteocles
and impulsive Polynices, and then two daughters.
I named the elder Antigone, and
Oedipus called our younger Ismene.
But when he learned his mother was his wife
such was his shame that Oedipus   60
with a gold brooch pin blinded himself in blood.

Now our two boys grown to manhood
keep their unhappy father closely guarded
in his dark prison, that such past
deeds might be forgotten by all of us.
Meanwhile, vexed, distraught, the father
has cast another curse upon his sons:

that these two offspring of his evil act
will reap his malediction with bloody swords.
Fearing to share the palace   70
where the gods might let that curse
come to pass, the brothers together
covenanted that Polynices, the younger,
would leave our land, so Eteocles
could wear the crown for just one year
and then alternate in power with his brother.
But Eteocles has refused to cede his throne
and banished Polynices from his home.
He went to Argos, married Adrastus'
daughter, and now has mustered Argive shields   80

in a huge army against our seven-gated walls,
claiming his brother's scepter as his own.

To pacify this strife I have pleaded with my sons to
meet in truce. According to the messenger I sent,
young Polynices has agreed,
so now I pray to Zeus in heaven's veiling light,
save us! Grant reconciliation to my brood!
Being so all wise, do not
forever let me and mine remain accursed.
(She exits. Enter Antigone and old servant)

OLD SERVANT
 Fair flower of your father's house,   90
 Antigone, though Jocasta has given you leave
 to go from your rooms and mount the palace roof
 to view this Argive army,
 stay down so I may scan the vista first.

 There's no real scandal if I am seen
 by common citizens, but you are a princess
 and must observe decorum. What I see
 below I'll tell you and all the words
 I heard the Argive soldiers speak
 when your mother sent me to Polynices   100
 to propose the truce.
(Intent on peering down, she climbs the wall.)
 Luckily, there are no citizens of Thebes
 below these walls. Climb up the cedar steps,
 and gaze out at the plain, along the stream,
 at this great gathering of Argive foes.

ANTIGONE
 Like a barefoot child upon these stairs
 I strain to see the spectacle below.

OLD SERVANT

> Battalion by battalion,
> observe how that hostile force
> maneuvers below.   110

ANTIGONE

> All the flash and glare of brass.

OLD SERVANT

> Polynices has armed himself
> abundantly, with countless
> horse and costly shields.

ANTIGONE

> Are the gates secure?
> The big clamped bolts
> made sure? Will these stone
> walls built by Amphion
> withstand that brash flood?

OLD SERVANT   .

> The city's safe inside.   120
> Have no fears for that.
> But look below. Their chief—
> do you know him?

ANTIGONE

> He marches before
> that whole army
> under a white-plumed helmet,
> his breast bound in brass,
> swinging his arm loosely.

OLD SERVANT

> That's their captain, princess.

ANTIGONE

    What do they call him? Where is he from?   130

OLD SERVANT

    Hippomedon from Lerma,
    Mycenean-born, a king.

ANTIGONE

    How bold he appears,
    and frightening, this giant
    whose shield is mirrored
    in the sun.

OLD SERVANT

    Do you see the other
    crossing Dirce now?

ANTIGONE

    His armor seems so foreign.
    Who is he?   140

OLD SERVANT

    Tydeus, son of
    Oeneus, an Aetolian,
    battle fired, all aglow.

ANTIGONE

    And tied by marriage
    to my brother, an ally,
    having won the sister
    of my brother's wife
    to be his bride.
    Those breast plates
    are barbaric, surely not   150
    of Greek design.

OLD SERVANT
　　These Aetolians march to battle
　　behind their shields, hurling
　　their spears like javelins.

ANTIGONE
　　How do you know so much
　　about war, old one?

OLD SERVANT
　　When your mother sent me
　　to Polynices to propose
　　the truce, I observed
　　all these soldiers,　　　　　　　　　　　　160
　　and I'd seen the Argives
　　in the field before.

ANTIGONE
　　Then tell me who is
　　that keen-eyed young warrior
　　with the long curls
　　standing beside Zethus'
　　sepulcher? He also
　　seems to be a leader.
　　Note the throng behind him.

OLD SERVANT
　　That's Atalanta's son,　　　　　　　　　　170
　　Parthenopaeus.

ANTIGONE
　　May Artemis with her bow
　　make a corpse of Parthenopaeus,
　　who came from so far away
　　to waste and ruin Thebes,
　　my city.

OLD SERVANT

    Try to remember, child,
    they too are only seeking
    justice. It may be that the gods
    will side with them.   180

ANTIGONE

    Is my brother Polynices
    down below?

OLD SERVANT

    Beside Adrastus, near
    the tomb of Niobe's
    seven virgin daughters.
    Can you see him now?

ANTIGONE

    I think I see his figure.
    How I wish I could fly
    to him and embrace
    that body with my arms,   190
    so long withheld from me
    in exile by Eteocles.
    Look how his armor gleams
    like morning light on water.

OLD SERVANT

    This truce should bring him
    back to you with joy.

ANTIGONE

    Who is that other in the chariot
    led by two white horses?

OLD SERVANT

    That's the prophet Amphiaraus,
    princess. He brings with him   200

sacrificial victims, many
blood offerings.

ANTIGONE

How calmly Amphiaraus
goads that team, one
horse at a time. Where
is Capaneus? He too
has hurled insults
and threats at Thebes.

OLD SERVANT

There! Don't you see?
He's measuring our walls,   210
gauging the scaling heights
of all our towers.

ANTIGONE

O Nemesis, deep thunder
before Zeus' zigzag lightening,
will Capaneus be that hero
to deliver Thebes'
captive daughters to
the women of Mycenae?
Never, never, never, Artemis,
will I bow down, a slave.   220

OLD SERVANT

Go inside again, take
shelter. Your desire
to see all has been attained.
Look! A throng of women
has come to these royal halls,
and since females love scandal
we're safe now only as long
as they can find no cause

for idle gossip. Even so
what they don't know they may   230
invent about you, princess.
Strange pleasure
women take to speak ill
of their own sisters.
(Exit old servant and Antigone. Enter Chorus of Phoenician women.)

CHORUS
From Phoenicia to Delphi,
in the thrall of Apollo,
chanting in his palace halls
like tides that swell
against the walls of Tyre,
I've traveled here   240
where Loxias inhabits
the always-present snow-
drifts on Parnassus. Across
Ionian seas our music
has been blown at chariot
speed over Sicily's
unharvested furrows
until the heavens recorded
this glorious sound.

As a beautiful gift to Apollo,   250
I've come to the land of Cadmus'
children, the noble sons of Agenor,
people of our own lineage,
to the towers of Laius,
like a golden statue,
arrayed for service to Apollo.
Let Castalia's fountain spray
my hair with shiny golden showers
that I braid in Phoebus' name.

Hail light-splashed rock!   260
Across your Bacchic peak
Dionysus haunts the cloven
tongue. Hail Parnassus,
that single Dionysian vine
that casts libation every
morning to the god with wine
from purple grapes. Hail
the cavern where the dragon
lived! Hail watch tower
of the archer-god! Hail   270
Parnassan ridges no mortal
has ever climbed! Fearless,
weaving a dance with our souls
to the immortal goddess,
we leave these fear-stricken
waters of Dirce for Apollo's groves.

Before the wall today,
Ares' hand ignites
the Theban slaughter torch.
God protect us from his will!   280
Friend with friend
unites in pain, and Phoenicia
in the ruin of this seven-gated
city shall console
a mourning nation. Drawn
from the heifer, Io's
brood, in lineage, is
one by blood.

Surrounding Thebes, Argive shields
with their flashing forecast blood,   290
but the war god will regret it
if the sons of our blind king

suffer this revenge.
Argos, I fear your massive strength,
fear that justice that the gods inflict
on Thebes for Polynices.
(Enter Polynices with drawn sword)

POLYNICES

I've slipped the bolted doors too easily
and made my way within these Theban walls
so that I fear if I am caught here
escape will prove impossible   300
except by shedding blood. Turning
every which way I can, my eyes alert
in case some treachery come, armed
with this sword, my hand will reassure
my desperate courage. Ha! Who goes there?
Am I afraid of sounds? To those who risk all,
all seems so perilous just as soon as they
find themselves on hostile ground, but I
trust her who begged me to come here
in a truce, my mother. And yet I must   310
also be cautious. Help is at hand,
the sacrificial hearths are near,
and there are citizens about.
I'll sheath my sword and ask these drabs
by the palace walls who they are. Women,
from what far land did you depart
for our Hellenic halls?

CHORUS

I was reared in Phoenicia. Agenor's
grandsons have sent me to Thebes
as battle spoil. When the sons   320
of Oedipus engaged in their old quarrel,
the Argives marched against this city.
Who are you to sneak inside the fortress?

POLYNICES

> Oedipus, son of Laius, was my father.
> My mother was Jocasta, Menoeceus' daughter.
> Thebans call me Polynices.

CHORUS

> You are my kinsman of Agenor's race,
> those rulers who despatched me here,
> and I bend my knees in obeisance
> in the manner of our people, King.   330
> You've come, at last, to the land of your fathers.
> Look now, the Queen is coming from the hall.
> Let all the palace portals ring.
> Jocasta, did you hear our call?
> Why have you waited so long to come out
> now and embrace your son, Polynices?

(Enter Jocasta.)

JOCASTA

> Your Tyrian accents hurt my ears, woman.
> See how my wobbly feet draw near.

(sees Polynices)

> O son, I see your face at last, after
> so long in exile—come, cast   340
> your arms about your mother
> and embrace me, form to form.

> Stoop to me, dear face, from above,
> and let your clustering locks unfurl
> love's banner against my neck.

> A tale told already were our hopes
> and dreams. What shall I tell you now?
> How can we bring back our former
> raptures? With a word? An embrace?
> In the swaying of our bodies? Our feet   350
> moving forward and back, twined in a dance?

Sweet son, through your brother's acts
you've forsaken your father's desolate
palace and are exiled. How we've ached
to see you again, all of Thebes aching.

Weeping, I cut my white hair short
and the chaff lies all about my feet.
No longer do I wear white.
My robes are the color of night.
Within these halls your blind old father   360
weeps and yearns for his noble sons,
severed from his love by their hatred,
my babe, your father, clings to his old remorse.

He would take his own life with a sword,
or hang himself on a noose from the roof
beams, mourning his malediction
on his children, bewailing his fate.

I hear you have taken a wife
in a stranger's house, making children
that gladden your life, but to me,   370
your mother, bring only more misery.
I never lit your bridal torch for you,
as joyful mothers do, nor did your
sister bathe your bride, nor did
our Theban maidens serenade her.
Your marrying felt like a curse
on this house and on Laius,
father's ancestor. Within these halls
news of your wedding came like doom.

All the tortures of this clashing   380
metal strife below have gathered
on my head with damned maledictions
on our ancient palace walls.

CHORUS
> For their ordeals of giving birth
> women love their offspring all the more.

POLYNICES
> All men love the countries of their births,
> and who does not is treacherous.
> I have come among my foes cautiously,
> though not with wisdom, mother,
> with misgivings, out of dread   390
> that my brother might betray our truce
> and have me murdered.
> Through your city I've passed, sword in hand, eye
> keen to every corner. Only your faith
> in our agreement drew me again to these
> ancestral walls. I came here full of sorrow—
> grieving to see my home so long abandoned,
> the altars to the gods, my childhood
> playing fields, and Dirce's spring.
> Having been banished wrongfully,   400
> for years to a strange land, I felt
> my eyes gush with tears.
>
> And when I saw your cropped hair
> and your mournful robes, I thought
> how woeful our calamities.
> Mother, terrible is this strife between brothers,
> and reconciliation seems hopeless.
> My ancient father in his halls
> of darkness, and my two sisters—
> what has my exile meant to them?   410

JOCASTA
> A god is ruining all of Oedipus' line,
> begun when I first wed your father
> under a god's curse, and you were born.

Why? If we must heed these godly whims,
how can I ask the thing that I most fear
and pain your soul when I want only peace?

POLYNICES

Ask, mother, don't be fearful. What
you wish to know is dear to me.

JOCASTA

Is exile truly wretchedness?

POLYNICES

It's terrible. Even harsher than the word   420
for banishment is living removed from Thebes.

JOCASTA

Why do you feel this way?

POLYNICES

An exile cannot speak his mind.

JOCASTA

Not to speak openly is a slave's life.

POLYNICES

The stupidities of those in power go unchallenged.

JOCASTA

Assenting to fools must be painful.

POLYNICES

Nature abhors the restraints that must be borne in exile.

JOCASTA

They say that exiles also feed on hope.

POLYNICES
Kind-eyed hope endures too much delay.

JOCASTA
And time lays bare the emptiness of hoping.   430

POLYNICES
Hope is all we have sustaining us in exile.

JOCASTA
Before you married, how did you keep yourself?

POLYNICES
Sometimes I ate, and sometimes I went hungry.

JOCASTA
Did friends of Oedipus help you?

POLYNICES
In bad times such friends vanish.

JOCASTA
Was your nobility esteemed?

POLYNICES
Poverty was a curse that fed off my nobility.

JOCASTA
Fatherland must be dear to men like you.

POLYNICES
So precious that it's hard to express the feeling.

JOCASTA
How did you come to Argos? Why?   440

POLYNICES

Fate summoned me.

JOCASTA

Wise fate! How did you win your bride?

POLYNICES

An oracle spoke to Adrastus.

JOCASTA

What was his prophecy?

POLYNICES

Your daughter shall wed a lion and a boar.

JOCASTA

What did you have in common with such brutes?

POLYNICES

One night I came to Adrastus' palace . . .

JOCASTA

Seeking a place of rest?

POLYNICES

Yes. But there was this other exile resting there.

JOCASTA

Who? What was his plight?   450

POLYNICES

His name was Tydeus, the son of Oeneus.

JOCASTA

And why did Adrastus liken you to beasts?

POLYNICES
> We fell to fighting over a bed . . .

JOCASTA
> Then he correctly understood the oracle.

POLYNICES
> He gave us each one of his daughters for a wife.

JOCASTA
> And are you happy with your bride?

POLYNICES
> I can find no fault with her even now.

JOCASTA
> How did you raise an army to follow you?

POLYNICES
> Adrastus promised his daughter's husbands—
> my brother-in-law Tydeus and me—that   460
> we should both be brought out of exile,
> myself first. Hence, many Mycenean chiefs
> are with me now and also, as that courtesy
> which saddens me to be so needy, many
> Danaans. So I'm arrayed in battle against
> my own countrymen but swear by all the gods
> I cannot willingly lift my spear
> against my father's house. Only you,
> mother, can assuage this rancor and
> unite again those who were one in blood.   470
> It's said wealth in men's eyes is always honored
> and of all things on earth is powerful.
> For this I've come, captaining countless
> spears, since my noble poverty was weak.

CHORUS
>   Eteocles is also coming to this parlay,
>   matriarch Jocasta, it's your duty
>   to bring your sons together through your words.
(Enter Eteocles.)

ETEOCLES
>   Here I am, mother—to honor you
>   I've come to talk. What do you want? Let
>   the talking start. For I have quit   480
>   my command post on the walls of Thebes
>   to hear your mediation, which,
>   I see, has also allowed safe passage
>   to my rebellious brother in our city.

JOCASTA
>   Be patient. Haste will not lead to justice.
>   But careful speaking often leads to wisdom.
>   Suppress your fierce gaze, that
>   look of passionate dread. This is your brother,
>   not the Gorgon's severed head.
(to Polynices)
>   Turn your face, Polynices, meet   490
>   Eteocles eye to eye so you can speak
>   more aptly, hear all he has to tell you.
>   This is my counsel to you who brings
>   here such hot wrath for his once-loved brother
>   when meeting him, eye to eye.
>   Narrow your thoughts to only what's at hand
>   and cherish no remembrance of old wrongs.
>
>   Polynices, you speak first,
>   for you have brought an army to our walls
>   and are feeling wronged, as you say.   500
>   Then let some god judge your case now
>   and reconcile ill feelings in both parties.

POLYNICES

I will speak plainly, without elaboration,
for justice needs no subtle sophistries
whereas the pleas of those who wrong another,
lacking truth, need gobs of cosmetic language.

I had regard for this great house
and took great care for Eteocles' sake
and mine to avoid the curse
uttered by Oedipus against his sons,   510
going of my own will from this realm
for one year by agreement so he could
rule the land, and I in turn in equal right
gain that sovereignty thereafter, avoiding
such hate and bloodshed with Eteocles
as may befall us now. He, in turn,
consented in the gods' sight and swore
a pledge that he no longer keeps, holding
onto the throne and my half patrimony.

Now I am preparing to right this wrong   520
with an army I've arrayed beneath the walls
and retake my house to live there again
as king, and force exile on him.

And if it's necessary I will bring
scaling ladders to assault these towers,
which I'll destroy by right. I ask
the gods to witness this—that
having justly honored our agreement,
I've been treated impiously, robbed
of fatherland unjustly. Point by point   530
I tell you these things, mother,
not wrapped in webs of words but shown
as simple naked truth, I think.

CHORUS

It seems to me he pleads quite soundly.

ETEOCLES

If wisdom and the truth were the same for all,
men would not fight one another.
But "justice,""equal rights"—these are mere words,
names, that have no palpable being.

Now, mother, I will speak without pretense:
I'd climb up to the stars or to the sun,   540
or plunge beneath the earth, if I could,
to maintain power here, more precious to me
than divinity. This precious power, mother,
I will not yield to any other when it's mine
to keep. It makes no sense for men
to throw away the good and grasp the worst.
Foul shame that he should come with arms,
lay waste the land, to win his heart's desire.
If I am cowed by Argive spears
and yield my scepter up to him to hold,   550
it's a reproach to Thebes. In quest of peace
one should not come with arms. Mother,
negotiations can accomplish more
than spears could ever bring to pass.
If he accepts things as they are
and lives in Thebes, he's safe here.
I'll accept his consent but will not yield
my throne to be a slave to him.

Therefore let fire and sword speak out now.
Yoke all the horses, let chariots fill the plain: 560
I shall not yield my sovereignty to him.
If one must do a wrong, it's best to do it
in pursuit of power. Virtue is weak otherwise.

JOCASTA

My son, old age doesn't make us feeble-minded.
Experience, more than youth, can lead to wisdom.
Ambition is the worst of deities, Eteocles;
don't embrace that Queen of Wrong.
She comes to many happy homes and cities
and won't depart until her acolytes are ruined.
She has made you mad, child, but it would be better   570
if you could woo justice and equality,
which brings together friend with friend,
cities with cities, allies in alliances.
Nature gave all men the law of equal rights,
and the more foes contest this ancient law
the more the dawn of hate is ushered in.
Equality ordains fair measurings for men
that equal weights and numbers are dealt out
just as the sun and the sightless face of night
show equally to humankind. Nor do they envy   580
either for their place in the diurnal round.
The sun and night are servants to all men:
Can't you also halve your patrimony and
share with Polynices? If not, where is justice?
Why must you prize such power—and enthrone injustice—
and count that some great thing? Are
the gods precious to you? It's only vanity
that you, with so much wealth, would
bring such strife. What do you gain?
Your profit is more loss: These words   590
to the wise man should suffice. Men
hold their possessions in this world
as stewards of the gifts of god.
Whenever—he will claim his own again;
the wealth we have is only for a day.
If I asked you now to choose whether
to be lord of Thebes or its protector,

would you say "lord"? If Polynices
should prevail with Argive spears
against our Cadmean strength, this city   600
will be ransacked and many captive maidens
raped and dishonored by the foe.
All the wealth you presently covet
will be a curse to Thebes, and you
will be Ambition's fool. I tell you this,
Eteocles, and to you, Polynices,
I say Adrastus gave you foolish leave
to march madly on Thebes and ravish her.
If you destroy this city—which the gods forbid—
what monuments will you build to Zeus?   610
How to give praise for ruining
your own home? And how inscribe your spoils
at Inachus? "Polynices has burnt Thebes
and to the Gods offers up these spoils"?
I hope you never win such Hellene fame.

And if your brother triumphs, leaving thousands dead,
what shall you say to Argos and Adrastus?
Will people say, "O cursed betrothal fixed
by you, Adrastus! Ruined for the sake of
Polynices' bride"? The outcome could be   620
bad in two respects. You could lose all
with Argos or fail in battle here.
Try to hold back your anger. When two
fools fight, the worst results take place.

CHORUS

O gods, keep them from this fight
and make the sons of Oedipus reunite.

ETEOCLES

It's much too late for talking,
just a waste of time. Never shall we

be as one again except by my decree.
I wear the crown of Thebes and wield   630
the scepter. Please stop your tedious
admonitions and let me rule. And as for
you, brother, leave this city now,
before I have you killed.

POLYNICES

You kill me? How? Are you so immortal
that you'd plunge your sword into my body
and manage to escape the same reward?

ETEOCLES

Do you see these hands of mine? You're
near enough.

POLYNICES

Your cowardly wealth will lose a lot in death.   640

ETEOCLES

You brought this army here to fight a coward?

POLYNICES

Better to be prudent than reckless.

ETEOCLES

You say that, knowing a truce protects you.

POLYNICES

It also protects you . . . Now once again
I claim my heritage and crown.

ETEOCLES

Your claims mean nothing to me. I
will stay here, in my own house,
on my own throne.

POLYNICES
>Taking what is not yours to keep.

ETEOCLES
>Leave us now.   650

POLYNICES
>O gods . . .

ETEOCLES
>He comes here only to destroy.

POLYNICES
>Hear me, brother!

ETEOCLES
>Why should they listen to your
>threats against this house,
>your home?

POLYNICES
>All you temples of the gods
>who ride white horses . . .

ETEOCLES
>They loathe your name.

POLYNICES
>I've been banished from my fatherland.   660

ETEOCLES
>Because you would destroy it.

POLYNICES
>Wrongfully banished, gods . . .

ETEOCLES

 Tell that to your Mycenean deities.

POLYNICES

 You are impious!

ETEOCLES

 But not my country's enemy, like you.

POLYNICES

 Having defrauded me and driven me forth.

ETEOCLES

 I'll murder you . . .

POLYNICES

 Father, did you hear that threat?

ETEOCLES

 He also knows what you are doing.

POLYNICES

 Mother, did you hear him?   670

ETEOCLES

 Such a plea is sacrilege.

POLYNICES

 Thebes, my city, listen . . .

ETEOCLES

 Go back to Argos, plead to Lerna's waters.

POLYNICES

 Don't worry. I'm leaving now. I want
 to thank you, mother.

ETEOCLES
> Leave this city! Go!

POLYNICES
> Before I leave I'd like to see our father.

ETEOCLES
> Never!

POLYNICES
> Then bring my sisters to me.

ETEOCLES
> You nevermore shall see them again.   680

POLYNICES
> O sisters!

ETEOCLES
> Why do you, their bitterest enemy,
> call for them?

POLYNICES
> Farewell, mother!

JOCASTA
> Son, I am too sad now to fare well.

POLYNICES
> And I can no longer be your son—

JOCASTA
> Women like me were born to suffer.

POLYNICES
> My brother's doing.

ETEOCLES
 For what you wish to do to me, brother!

POLYNICES
 Where can we meet before these towers?   690

ETEOCLES
 Why do you ask me that?

POLYNICES
 There I will slay you.

ETEOCLES
 Just what I want to hear you say!

JOCASTA
 O my sons, will you bring me even more grief?

POLYNICES
 You'll see, mother.

JOCASTA
 Run from your father's curse.

ETEOCLES
 Let ruin seize this house!

POLYNICES
 Soon my bloody sword will hide no longer.
 Earth that nursed me, now I call you witness
 and all you gods in heaven, witness   700
 how I was driven from my house by
 shameful acts, treated like a slave
 by our father's other son, Eteocles.
 Whatever happens, Thebans, don't blame me
 for treacheries inflicted by this tyrant;

blame him, Eteocles. I did not come here
willingly. Farewell, Apollo, highway king,
farewell, and palace bowers farewell too.
Farewell to friends from youth, and statues
of the gods, for I may not address you　　　　　710
all again. Though I still live in hope,
in which I trust that I will slay Eteocles
and afterward mount the throne of Thebes.

ETEOCLES

Our father named you "Man of many feuds,"
Polynices, with heavenly prescience.
Leave us now!
(Exit Polynices.)

CHORUS

Cadmus to this fertile plain
came from Tyre with the heifer
who went lame and fell to earth,
as the oracle said it would,　　　　　720
and here, where Dirce's waters flow,
Thebes at last was given birth,
as Bacchus' mother married Zeus
where the wheat was all aglow.

Bacchus, even though a child,
and tendriled in the twining ivy,
saw the dancing Theban girls,
heard the women call his name.

Near Ares' spring a dragon
kept the fountain's hallowed border,　　　　　730
and the glare of fiery eyes
pulsing with a wandering keenness
guarded all that mirrored greenness.
when Cadmus came to purify
his body in that Dircean flood.

With his monster-slaying arm
he hurled a boulder at the head
and brought the dragon to great harm,
sowing teeth among the furrows
at Pallas' unmothered bidding,   740
until the spinning globe sent up
Theban warriors armor-clad
to drench earth's breast with blood
beneath the shimmering winds of heaven.

Is anything too hard for the gods?
Epaphus, Io's child, I call—
son of our mother and of Zeus—
come now to defend this land!
Your descendants founded it,
and Kore and Demeter own it,   750
and rule all this, the earth.
Send us goddesses of the torch,
defend us from their acts of war.

ETEOCLES *(to a servant)*
Go and bring me Creon, Menoeceus' son,
the brother of Jocasta, my own mother.
I would consult with him on private
matters, and state affairs, before
I go to fight . . .
(glances stage right)
But wait! He has saved
you such trouble, and comes   760
before I sent for him.
(Creon enters.)

CREON
I've been wandering all about trying to see you, King,
passing all the Cadmean gates and guards,
and never once able to find Eteocles anywhere.

ETEOCLES

I'm glad to see you, Creon.
My talk with Polynices was of little worth.
He wanted war, not peace.

CREON

Your mother's son desires more than Thebes.
He trusts Adrastus and his new army.
Let's leave this to the gods. I've   770
other news I must pass on to you.

ETEOCLES

What can such be? Your drift is dark.

CREON

We have an Argive prisoner at hand.

ETEOCLES

What does he have to say to us?

CREON

The Argive troops will shortly circle Thebes
and weave their net of spears like armor.

ETEOCLES

Then we shall have to meet them on the open plain.

CREON

Where? How? Don't be rash, nephew.

ETEOCLES

We'll cross the trenches to fight on open land.

CREON

We are too few, and they're a multitude.   780

ETEOCLES

Though bold, I think, only in their speech.

CREON

Argos' strength is awesome to the Greeks.

ETEOCLES

Their corpses soon will cover the whole plain.

CREON

That I wish, but I am fearful of such slaughter.

ETEOCLES

I will not keep my troops inside these walls.

CREON

Victory comes with wise advice.

ETEOCLES

What would you have me do otherwise?

CREON

Don't risk your whole army with one attack.

ETEOCLES

Suppose we fell on them by night?

CREON

If, when you failed, you could return here safe . . .   790

ETEOCLES

Night is to our advantage. It furthers our attack.

CREON

Dread comes to those who fail in darkness.

ETEOCLES

Perhaps a spear attack while they are eating.

CREON

Surprise is not the same as victory.

ETEOCLES

Dirce's flow should hamper their retreating.

CREON

It's better that we hold out here in safety.

ETEOCLES

What if we rode against the Argive camp?

CREON

They're well walled in by chariots and shields.

ETEOCLES

What would you have me do, surrender?

CREON

Take good advice, though you are very clever.   800

ETEOCLES

Who has knowledge better than my own?

CREON

I'm told that seven stalwarts stand with Polynices.

ETEOCLES

To do what? Seven is a puny onslaught.

CREON

And each will bring a charge against Thebes' gates.

TEOCLES

What of it? I will not despair.

CREON

Choose seven of our best to guard each gate.

TEOCLES

To fight with single spears?

CREON

To lead our soldiers. Only choose the strongest . . .

TEOCLES

So as to keep them from our walls?

CREON

And give them good lieutenants; one man   810
cannot lead everyone.

TEOCLES

Shall I choose valorous men, or those of prudent wits?

CREON

Choose both. Without both, each is nothing.

TEOCLES

I'll do it. Go to the seven towers
and plant good men at the gates,
as you say, champion against champion,
ready for their foes. I don't have time
to tell you every name so long as
Polynices camps beyond our walls.
But I will do this, so my arm will not   820
be idle. God, grant I meet my brother
face to face, fight him hand to hand

and slay him there, who came only
to destroy Thebes. As for my sister
Antigone's marriage to your son,
Haemon—if I fail in this endeavor,
that's for you to bring about. I verify
their earlier betrothal. You are my
mother's brother. Why waste words?

Take care of her, for my sake and   830
for yours. My remorseful father's
folly was to blind himself. I can't extol such
acts, and his curse on us may yet
slay all of us in battle.

One thing more: we
should send one of our own to fetch
Tiresias and ask the seer what he
foresees for us. Your son, Menoeceus,
named after your own father, should go,
for the seer will surely speak with your son,   840
whereas he hates me now for hating all
his blameful prophecies. I lay one further
charge on you, uncle, and on our city—
that if we win, Polynices not be
buried here in Thebes. Whoever seeks
to bury him here must die, no matter
who. Now I must arm myself to win this
fight so justice will prevail
through victory, and pray to Prudence,
kindest of the goddesses, to save our city.   850
(Exit Eteocles.)

CHORUS

Ares, bringer of troubles, of blood and death,
why do you shirk the feasts of the revelry king?
Not for you the dancing, the circles of beautiful
virgins when they are crowned. You do not toss

your tresses about and sing to the breathing flutes.
With war lust for Theban blood, you bring
the army of Argos around us, dance
the dance without music. When the thyrsus
whirls and the fawnskins reel you are
not found idling beside Ismenus' waters   860
but appear with thunder, the clashing
of metal bits, chariots, and warhorse
footfalls, to urge these Argives to hate
the sons of this dragon-state with a
rush of steeds, arrayed in bronze,
battering our stone walls with a fearful
array. War is a terrible goddess
to have planted such anguish among
our Labdacid kin in this land.

Adored glade of Artemis, O Cithaeron,   870
that wears snow upon your body,
I wish you had not rescued Jocasta's son
and brought that lecherous foundling to be reared
as Oedipus, this swollen foot, blinded for life
by a golden pin—and I wish
that the winged Sphinx,
the mountain maid's portent of grief,
had never sung her songs to Oedipus.
Such music was no music at all! She dragged
this riddled youth to sunlit cloudland, she   880
whom Hades from the dens of the dead soon
sped against the children of Cadmus.
Now a new curse flames in Theban halls
as between these brothers when
the seeds of hell are blossoming red.
Such utter shame to bear in honor's name,
the stain of their begetter
who took his parent to his bed.
(moves to center stage)

Even in my foreign home I
heard news of that race   890
that sprang up from the dragon's teeth,
the Thebans' oldest shame.
When Cadmus married Harmonia
they appeared at the wedding,
and the walls of Thebes rose up
to the strains of Amphion's lyre,
halfway between the streams
of Dirce and Ismenus
which pour their dreamlike flows
over that green-rich plain.   900
My horned forebear, Io, ancestored
all the kings of Thebes.
This city has been governed
by various rulers, but always
has stood strong and tall,
decked with the war god's crowns
(Enter Tiresias led by his daughter, with Menoeceus.)

TIRESIAS

Lead on, child. As stars for mariners,
you are the eyes for my sightless feet.
Place me on level ground so I won't stumble.
I am very old and weak. Guard these tablets   910
on which I drew my prophecies when I
was listening to the oracle-birds.
Menoeceus, Creon's child, how far
away from us is your father in the city?
My knees are faint. I've traveled far
and do not have much strength.

CREON

Be assured, Tiresias, you're with friends now.
Hold onto him, son. Mule carts and ancient feet
need to be propped up by a strong young arm.

TIRESIAS

>Why this summons, Creon,   920
>now?

CREON

>Rest easy. Take your time. Collect your strength,
>draw your breath, shrug off the weariness of travel.

TIRESIAS

>I am truly very weary, since only yesterday
>I returned from king Erechtheus' sons.
>There, too, was fighting against the spears of Eumolpus,
>and I gave victory to the children of Cecrops,
>from the spoils of which I have been given
>this golden crown by the victors as my reward.

CREON

>Your victory crown must be a good omen.   930
>We're now besieged by danger, as you know,
>from the Danaans, and Thebes is prepared
>to struggle. Clad in warrior armor, king
>Eteocles has gone off even now to
>challenge Mycenae's might. Before he left
>he told me to inquire of you, ancient,
>what deeds we shall do to best deliver Thebes?

TIRESIAS

>As far as Eteocles is concerned, I must
>not say a word but, as you've asked me,
>Creon, I will tell you that Thebes has   940
>long been ill since Laius spawned a son
>against god's will, and brought to life
>impulsive Oedipus, who had incest with
>his dead father's wife. Those bloody sockets
>that were his eyes are the gods' most cruel
>warning to all of Greece. When his two sons

tried in the fullness of time to hide his shame
they angered the gods all the more
by granting the old reprobate king—
now ailing and dishonored—   950
no freedom, nor the liberty to leave Thebes,
and that stung the wretch to such an angry fury
that he cursed them terribly. What
did I tell them then to do?
From these sons all I got was hatred.
But now a mutual slaughter looms
and many corpses threaten to pile up
upon this plain, transfixed by Argive
and our Cadmean shafts; Thebes will
endure a bitter mourning. Grief! My poor city,   960
you will be buried with them
unless you listen to my words. It
would be best that none of this cursed
family remain in Thebes as citizens or
nobles. They are possessed of evil
fortune and doomed to destroy this city.
But there is still one other way to save
Thebes, which it is not even safe for me
to mention to you, it being so bitter to
a man of power like you. I'm going now. Farewell.   970
What must happen will. I'm only one man
in a multitude and will accept whatever
happens. There's nothing else I can do.
(turns to go)

CREON
　　Stay here, old man.

TIRESIAS
　　Let go of me.

CREON
　　Stay, don't flee!

TIRESIAS

> Your fortunes flee, not I!

CREON

> Tell us what we can do to be safe.

TIRESIAS

> Although you say it, I don't think you mean it.

CREON

> Not wish to save my fatherland? 980

TIRESIAS

> You really want to know?

CREON

> Of course! How can I prove my earnestness?

TIRESIAS

> Then you shall hear what you must do.
> But I would first make certain that your son,
> Menoeceus, who brought me here, is
> out of hearing range.

CREON

> He's by your side, old man.

TIRESIAS

> Have him remove himself while we
> are speaking.

CREON

> He's my son. He'll keep our secrets. 990

TIRESIAS

> You wish me to speak in front of him?

CREON

    Yes. He also cares about our safety.

TIRESIAS

    Then hear what I must tell you.
    You will save Thebes from destruction
    only if you sacrifice Menoeceus.
    Kill your son for Thebes! Since you asked to know . . .

CREON

    What are you saying? How?

TIRESIAS

    It's foredoomed that you must do this.

CREON

    Such misery in this one prophecy!

TIRESIAS

    Misery for you, but salvation for Thebes.   1000

CREON

    I do not hear you! Cannot listen! Leave me!

TIRESIAS

    A moment ago he was a different man. My
    message made him flinch.

CREON

    Go in peace; I don't want your warnings.

TIRESIAS

    And truth should die because you are unhappy?

CREON *(kneeling)*

    By your knees and by your long white beard . . .

TIRESIAS

Why kneel to me? You're pleading for your own ruin.

CREON

Shut up! Don't let the city hear you.

TIRESIAS

I will not hold my tongue! It's a sin.

CREON

What will you do to me? You'd slay my son?   1010

TIRESIAS

Others will. I only know and speak.

CREON

How were we chosen for this curse?

TIRESIAS

Fair question! You are right to ask me that.
In that den where the earth-born dragon dwelt—
who watches over Dirce's streams—your boy
must be slaughtered, and this blood sacrifice
for the crime of Cadmus must be made to Ares,
who feels anger for all the kin
of dragon-slaying Cadmus. Do this now
and Ares will become your ally.   1020

Thus, if earth gives fruit for fruit, and for
her own offspring human blood, then all
Thebes shall be friendly to you, appeasing
Ares, who produced that golden helmeted
crop of men from the dragon's teeth. It's said
one of that race, a child of the dragon's
jaws, must die for Thebes. You are
the one survivor of that line,

and pure-blooded, you and your sons,
on both sides. Haemon is saved because   1030
he is betrothed, if unwedded,
and still a virgin. Menoeceus belongs
to none except Thebes, and by dying
he could save your fatherland,
and yield a bitter return to
Adrastus and the Argive army, drawing
the dark of night across their eyes,
making Thebes glorious. So you have a choice:
to save your city or your son.

(to his daughter)

Lead me homeward now, child.   1040
Whoever uses the diviner's art is foolish.
If he augurs, evil events he hates will come
to those to whom he makes his prophecy.
But, if he pities them and lies,
he wrongs the gods. Apollo ought to be
the only prophet of the human race
because he need fear none.

(Exit Tiresias and his daughter.)

CHORUS

Why are you silent, Creon?
Why do you not speak?
Our consternation is   1050
no less than yours.

CREON

What can I say? My answer clearly is
never will I be so miserable
as offer up my son to save this city.

(to his son)

Don't listen to these feckless soothsayers.
Hurry from Thebes. Flee with all speed.
Tiresias will visit all the gates

and seek to influence all their stalwart
captains to stay you, but we'll forestall him.
Now you are safe. But hurry. If you lag,   1060
your father is undone, and you will die.

MENOECEUS
Where shall I flee? What city? Where do
I have friends?

CREON
Get as far away from here as you can.

MENOECEUS
Tell me where and I will go.

CREON
Beyond Delphi . . .

MENOECEUS
Where?

CREON
To Aetolia.

MENOECEUS
Where shall I find haven there?

CREON
On Thesprotia's soil.   1070

MENOECEUS
On Dodona's hallowed floor?

CREON
Just so.

MENOECEUS
>Who will be my protector there?

CREON
>The god who speeds you.

MENOECEUS
>How will I get by?

CREON
>I'll find you gold.

MENOECEUS
>I will do as you say, father,
>in haste. Now I'll go to your sister,
>Jocasta, who nurtured me from
>her own bosom when I was an orphan,   1080
>alone, just to say farewell to her
>before I flee. Let me pass inside,
>and do not hinder me.

(Exit Creon.)

MENOECEUS *(to the Chorus)*
>I've quieted my father's fears with guile,
>women, to hasten to my own desires.
>He would have me flee, robbing Thebes
>of hope, branding me a coward. In time
>I might be forgiven for such cowardice,
>but how could I forgive myself, having
>betrayed the city of my birth?   1090
>Never doubt that I will save my Thebes
>and give my soul to death. It would be
>shameful if the stalwarts not constrained
>by oracles stood shoulder to shoulder,
>not fearing death, before the towers

of our city while I, betraying that
same city of my father and my brother,
fled from this place to live in shame
wherever else I dwelt.

By star-throned Zeus, by Ares lord of war,   1100
who as the kingly god of Thebes installed
the dragon's brood that sowed earth's womb,
I will leave now to stand upon the ramparts,
and over the dragon's gloomy den will slay
myself and make my city free. Agreed!

I leave to give my city no mean gift.
My life will save this land from ruin.
If all men offered all their goodness
to their cities' commonweals, cities
would thrive with joys in common.   1110
(Exit Menoeceus.)

CHORUS

You came, O doomed thing with wings
and fruit of Earth's laboring.
Begotten by that burrowing worm of gloom,
you sprang on Cadmus' sons
with death and moanings for the dead.

Half virgin, half a beast,
Sphinx of roving pinions,
with red talons, from that
flesh-ravening feast, shrieking fury,
you snatched these youths   1120
from Dirce's meadow. You brought
a song that knows no music, anguish
upon the land, sorrows, blood,
so bloody was that god
who brought these things to pass.

Mourning mothers, weeping maidens,
jammed our homes with grief, with
wailing from one to another in the
city, and loud thunder when the winged
bird seized one of our city's youths.   1130

At last misbegotten Oedipus
arrived in Thebes from Pytho,
and, at first, we were glad
but later we grieved.
He solved the three-legged
riddle, married and took to bed
his own mother. He corrupted
Thebes and cursed his misbegotten
sons to fight each other. Praise
then him who shall die to save   1140
this city. He leaves his father,
Creon, a despairing love. But
preserves the crown of this
seven-gated city. May such a
noble son make us mothers,
of sons as good as he, Pallas,
you for whom the sudden stone
was thrown by Cadmus, spilling
dragon's blood which brought
the curse of god upon this place,   1150
and slaughter with it.

(Enter Messenger.)

MESSENGER

Hello! Who stands beside the palace gate?
Open it, and bring Jocasta to me.
Hello, you! It's late, but please step
forward. Listen to me, notorious wife
of Oedipus. Stop your crying.

(Enter Jocasta.)

JOCASTA

> Friend! Friend! As you are one of my son's
> soldiers, do you come with bad news
> of Eteocles' death? What word do you
> bring? Is my son alive or dead?   1160
> Tell me the truth. Is he dead?

MESSENGER

> He's alive. Don't be so fearful.

JOCASTA

> How are our seven gates holding back such enemies?

MESSENGER

> They stand unbroken.

JOCASTA

> Are they in danger?

MESSENGER

> Almost in jeopardy, but Cadmean strength
> holds out against Mycenean spears.

JOCASTA

> What about Polynices? Is my other
> son alive?

MESSENGER

> Both of your sons still breathe.   1170

JOCASTA

> Bless you! When we were so besieged
> how did we force the Argives
> from our gates? Tell me, so I
> may please blind old Tiresias,
> who waits inside for news.

MESSENGER

When Creon's son climbed up the tower
and thrust his black-handled sword
across his throat, dying to save
his city, seven stalwart bands
went to the seven gates to watch   1180
and guard against the Argive spears.
Eteocles sent horseman against their
horsemen, and infantry with shields,
so where the wall was weakest
he was guarding it. From the highest
citadel we saw the white-shielded
men of Argos leave Teumesus and rush
the ditch to set our city on fire.
The trumpet swelled, and paeans shrilled.

Then Parthenopaeus, the huntress' son,   1190
led troops with shields in ranks
against the Neitian Gate. On his
shield was the emblem of his house,
Atalanta slaying the Aetolian boar.
Against the gate of Proteus, meanwhile,
came Amphiaraus, man of sacrifices
with his car of victims, and no heraldry
upon his shield. Against the gate of
Ogygia the lord Hippomedon
charged with a logo in the middle of his shield   1200
of the All-Seeing one with so many eyes
that, as the stars came out, they were veiled
with night, as he would be when he was slain.

Tydeus went against the Gate of Homole
with his shield draped in a lion's hide,
all shaggy-haired, and Titan Prometheus
carried a torch with him to burn our city.

At the Fountain Gate it was your
Polynices who led their charge. His shield
was blazoned with the racing steeds of Potniae   1210
in a frenzy, spun by a pivot near the
handle grip that whirled it crazily about.
And when Capaneus led a force against
the Electran Gate, the iron markings
on his shield were of an earth-born
giant carrying on his shoulders a
whole town wrestled from its found-
ations, suggesting what our Thebes
might soon endure. Adrastus
took on the seventh gate, with a shield   1220
painted with a hundred vipers, and from his
left arm swung the Argive Hydra, and these same
snakes with gnashing jaws were snatching
Cadmus' children from our walls.

From where I stood I witnessed this
when I was sent to give each gate the
password, and saw them fight with
bows and javelins, and then with
catapults careening stones, and
sling shots. When we'd prevailed,   1230
Tydeus suddenly shouted with your son,
"Sons of the Danaans, don't delay!

"Before they injure you, assault their
gates with light armed horses and
chariots." And none hung back,
soon as they heard this cry. With
heads bashed and bloodied, many
of their men fell, and on our side,
too, men dove from our walls into
the rocky seas of death, drenching   1240
that thirsty soil with streams of gore.

Only Atalanta's son, the Arcadian,
who was not an Argive, rushed at
our gates again, commanding those
with fire and double axes to follow
him, meaning to raze the city, but
the sea-god's son, Polyclemenus,
dropped a wagon-load of stone
from a battlement down against his
shield, and split his yellow head,   1250
rent the knittings of his skull,
so that his cheeks were overwhelmed
with blood. He'll bring no living presence
back to the archer queen, his maiden
mother. Seeing this gate had been
defended, Eteocles went on to the
next, where Tydeus and many with shields
beside him were hurling Aetolian spears
against our first lines of defense,
who fled in panic. But our king   1260
rallied them, like a hunter calling
back his hounds, so that they manned
those walls again, and we pressed on
to other gates, the mischief being stayed.

How should I tell you of the fate
of raging Capaneus? Grasping
a long scaling ladder, he and his
troops climbed up, boasting
that not even the most awful fires of Zeus
would deter him from overturning Thebes.   1270
As we pelted him with stones he
cried all this, and still he climbed,
cowering behind his shield, step after
step, rung after rung, and when he reached
the cornice of the wall he was struck
by lightning, and the whole earth

below rang out, as his body flew off the
ladder, his limbs spread-eagled, hair
streaming heavenward while his blood
rained on the ground: he spun   1280
like Ixion on his wheel, whirled, and fell
to earth, a burning corpse. Seeing that
Zeus was now his enemy, Adrastus drew
his army back behind the ditch,
and from our gates we sent our chariots
and infantry with leveled spears
who ran among that Argive disarray
creating murderous turmoil. Men died,
or fell from chariots beneath
their wheels, were ground by axles,   1290
and everywhere a confusion of dead bodies.

So it seems today we've vanquished those
who tried to topple Thebes, but if
the city was so lucky, it was godly luck:
A god's hand rescued Thebes today.

CHORUS

Victory is glorious. May we be so blest
by the gods with a second triumph.

JOCASTA

The gods and Fate deal fairly with Thebes:
my own sons live and the land has escaped
great harm. Only Creon has received evil   1300
tidings from my marriage with Oedipus.
Poor brother, bereft of his young son,
a sacrifice for Thebes. How he must grieve.
But tell me now what's likely to happen next.
What do my warring sons intend to do?

MESSENGER

No more questions, please. You have heard well.

JOCASTA

Now I'm suspicious. What do you mean to say?

MESSENGER

Know only that your sons are safe.

JOCASTA

But will they stay that way?

MESSENGER

Let me go. Eteocles needs me.   1310

JOCASTA

You're hiding something from me.

MESSENGER

I will not blend good news with evil tidings.

JOCASTA

You will, or else grow wings and fly away.

MESSENGER

Why don't you let me take my leave after
only giving you good news? Why want the rest?
Your two sons are planning combat man to
man, apart from all their troops—
an act of desperation! To their soldiers,
Argives as well as Cadmeans, they declare
what god would leave unsaid. Eteocles   1320
from a lofty tower, having demanded silence,
said, "O battle chiefs of Hellas, lords
of the Danaans who have trekked here,
and also Cadmeans—do not yield up your lives
for Polynices, nor sell them in my cause,
for I will free you of such mortal risks,
and fight alone against my rebel brother.

If I kill him this palace will stay mine.
And if I lose the fight, I yield the throne
to him. Forbear the struggle, Argives,   1330
and return to your sweet land, unharmed.
Too many are already slain in combat."

So he spoke. Polynices then, your son,
leaped from his ranks and hurled the challenge
back; and all the Argives cheered him on,
and also Cadmeans, thinking he did right,
made truce with their foe. And on that plain
their chiefs took oaths that they would
keep that truce. Then the two sons of
ancient Oedipus straightaway donned   1340
their brazen armor, assisted by
their friends, the king by Theban lords,
and Polynices by the Danaan nobles.
Then they stood there, gleaming in their
armor, each breathing fiercely at his
foe, as though daring him to hurl his
spear, while their friends encircled
them, with heartening words such as:
"It is up to you, Polynices, to erect
the triumph statue to the god Zeus,   1350
and give Argos fame." And to Eteocles,
"You're fighting now for Thebes,
and in your triumph you will raise
her scepter high." So they were cheered
and urged to fight, and the priests
slew the sacrificial lamb and on the fire
marked the points of flame, betokening
possible victory or defeat in the reek
of burning flesh. Now they will fight,
and if you have power still or cunning   1360
words or charms, go and pluck your sons
from this grim combat. There's great

danger. If you should lose both sons
today, your only prize will be your tears.
(Exit Messenger.)

JOCASTA

Antigone, come outside the house.
The gods have made it so there's no
help coming to you in dancing and
in maiden toil. Your brave brothers
are about to kill each other, reeling
in combat only I can stop from happening.   1370

ANTIGONE

Mother, what terror has you now crying
out like this in front of the palace?

JOCASTA

Your brothers are about to die.

ANTIGONE

What?

JOCASTA

They meet in combat face to face.

ANTIGONE

What can we say?

JOCASTA

Hard words. Now follow me.

ANTIGONE

Where to from my chamber?

JOCASTA

Among the armies.

ANTIGONE
    I fear those crowds.   1380

JOCASTA
    It's no use being modest now.

ANTIGONE
    What can I do?

JOCASTA
    Deter your brothers' spears.

ANTIGONE
    How, mother?

JOCASTA
    Fall at their feet with me.

ANTIGONE
    Lead me. We should not delay.

JOCASTA
    Hurry! Hurry! If I can postpone
    my children fighting face to face,
    the light of life is mine and
    grace. And if I find them slain,   1390
    I'll die on bloody ground beside them.
(*Exits.*)

CHORUS
    Woe, woe my shuddering flesh!
    I pity the mother in her misery:
    Two sons, killed by each other,
    in their blood will lie.

Woe, anguish, dismay!
Zeus, Earth—to you I pray!
Blood shed by a brother, a cleft
shield, a throat pierced?
Alas for their sufferings . . .   1400
Which corpse shall I lament?

Woe, woe, twin beasts in a
murderous mood. Shaking with
battle lust they stood, and soon
brother sheds brother's blood.
How awful that they should fight!
I mourn their encounter with
alien words chanted. Tears
for the dead, and cries of
lamentation. Murder is near at hand,   1410
in the balance slaughter, vengeance.

And I see Creon coming with clouded brow
toward this palace, I'll stop wailing now.
(Enter Creon, with attendants, bearing the body of Menoeceus.)

CREON
What shall I do? Should my tears lament
my own fate, or the fate of cursed Thebes?
My son is dead. He died for Thebes,
winning himself a glorious name, and woe for me.
From the dragon rocks I carried him
back just now to our mourning household.

In my old age I come for my aged   1420
sister, Jocasta, to bathe him and lay
the corpse out for his funeral rites.
We who are not yet dead must respect
the dead, honoring the gods below.

CHORUS

> Your sister's fled the palace
> with her child, Antigone.

CREON

> Where? Why did they rush off? Tell me.

CHORUS

> She learned her sons were fighting face
> to face for possession of these royal halls.

CREON

> What are you telling me? I'd not heard this   1430
> when I was so busy tending to my son's body.

CHORUS

> Some time ago she left here. Surely combat
> between the sons of Oedipus is ended now.

CREON *(glancing up and pointing)*

> He who comes with downcast face,
> this messenger, may testify to that.

(Enter Messenger.)

MESSENGER

> The news I bring is sorrow-laden. Woe is me!

CREON

> Your prologue is so gloomy we must be vanquished.

MESSENGER

> Worse in woe than that is my burdensome dismay.

CREON

> One calamity after the next! What's your news?

CHORUS

> Both your sister's sons are dead.   1440

CREON

> Alas! You bring great misery to me and Thebes.
> House of Oedipus, have you heard this
> news? In common doom your sons have
> slain each other!

CHORUS

> This royal house would weep if it could
> understand.

CREON

> O heavy fate. No suffering can be worse.

MESSENGER

> There's more you do not know.

CREON

> What could be worse?

MESSENGER

> Your sister died with her two sons.   1450

CHORUS

> Let the lamentations begin, the
> blows of mourning fall.

CREON

> Miserable Jocasta, what an ending to your
> life, and to that marriage riddled with
> the Sphinx's curse. How did her two
> sons die? How did that curse of Oedipus
> destroy them?

MESSENGER

You know these walls protected us against
their first forays, for they were not so far
away you could not see the fighting. When   1460
they were finally clad in battle armor,
the sons of Oedipus strode into that space
beyond the walls and stood like metal gods,
waiting for their single combat to begin.

Gazing toward Argos, Polynices prayed:
"Queen Hera—I'm your votary since I wed
the daughter of Adrastus and came to live
in Argos. Grant that I kill my brother
and stain my warring hand with victory blood!"
The shameful crown he begged was dead   1470
Eteocles'. Monstrous this fate that brought
tears to our eyes. Men seemed ashamed to
meet each other's gaze. Then the king,
his brother, Eteocles prayed to Pallas
of the golden shield: "Daughter of Zeus,
grant that this spear from my hand speed
toward my brother's breast and slay him
who came here to destroy this land."

The trumpet like a torch blared out,
the herald of their bloody onslaught,   1480
and they rushed at each other fiercely
like wild boars whose savage teeth
are sharpened, and clashed again, with foam
slathering down their beards. Crouching
behind their shields, they lunged with spears
so that steel points were dashed aside,
and if, beyond a rim, the other's eye
peered out, he thrust his spear again,
hoping to blind his brother with his point.
Cunningly, through eyelets in their shields,   1490

both saw and parried and evaded harm,
while we who watched sweated with our fears
that sooner or later such a harm might come.
When Eteocles slipped a little on a stone,
his leg spread out beneath his shield
showing the flesh toward which his brother
lunged to strike, the mark offered to his
spear, and Argive steel passed through his
calf, and all the sons of Danaus cheered.
But by that effort Polynices bared his   1500
shoulder, and then his brother struck
him in the breast with a strong thrust
and pierced him through, and Thebans cheered.
His spear head broke off short, so that he
lost his lance and fell back step by step,
then found a rock and hurled it hard,
breaking Polynices' spear. Now their fight
was equal once again as both were spearless,
so, seizing swords, they closed again and
clashed, swords against shields, and what   1510
a noise raged from the stormy clamor of
their fight. Having been once in Thessaly,
Eteocles knew an old Thessalian stunt:
eyeing his foe's waist, he fell back on his
left foot, and then leaped forward with
his right foot foremost, and plunged his
sword through Polynices' navel, and pierced
him to the spine so his ribs and belly
buckled forward and he fell, vomiting
blood. Not noticing his own risk, the   1520
victor plunged his sword into the earth
and began to strip his dying brother's armor,
but the dying man still grasped a weapon.
When Eteocles bent above him, Polynices
plunged his blade into his heart,
so that both died almost in the same instant,

side by side, gnashing their teeth in dust,
twinned in mortality, the victor still in doubt.

CHORUS

Woe to you, Oedipus, for your terrible losses.
Some god has now fulfilled your awful curses.   1530

MESSENGER

Hold off and listen to what woes remain to tell.
Even as her fallen sons were dying, Jocasta
rushed upon this scene, she and Antigone
in haste, and seeing they were stricken
by such wounds, she cried, "I have come too late!"
Then, falling on each son in turn, she wept and
moaned, while their sister by her side, cried out,
"Dear brethren, supporters of our mother, you've
betrayed my marriage hopes." With one dying gasp
heaving from his breast, King Eteocles heard   1540
his mother, touched her with a clammy hand,
said nothing, but from his eyes the tears spoke,
giving her tokens of his love, and Polynices,
gazing on the pair, said, "Mother, we're dying.
I pity you, and you my sister, and my foe,
my brother, whom I murdered, though I loved
him always. Bury me in our native soil, mother,
sister. Persuade the angry city to allow
me this much of our territory, though I
die and lose my home, then close my eyelids   1550
with your hand, mother, and farewell, darkness
wraps me." Thus, together, they both breathed their last.

And when Jocasta witnessed this, in grief she
snatched a sword from one who'd fallen and
drove the blade through her own neck, so now
she lies with her beloved boys in death.
Afterward, we were on our feet crying out

victory, and they said that their lord was our
conqueror, and there was strife between the
stalwarts, they shouting, "Polynices struck   1560
his spear first," and we "that both are dead
so none could be victorious."

Antigone alone was left alive.
Then Argives rushed at us with swords and spears,
but we were still protected by our shields
and could forestall that host, and fell on them
unprotected by their shields. None could withstand
our charge, and fled that plain, leaving many dead
streaming with blood. So victors in that fight
we raised a victory trophy up to Zeus, and   1570
some stripped shields from off that Argive host
and sent them back within our battlements.
And others are returning with Antigone,
bearing the two dead brothers for their friends
to mourn them, and the war for Thebes has ended
happily for some, but sadly nonetheless.
*(Enter procession, with Antigone and attendants bearing the bodies of
her brothers and Jocasta.)*

CHORUS

No need to recite the city's grief.
You may see the three dead bodies
on their way to the palace, in death as
one when into darkness they have gone.   1580

ANTIGONE

On my delicate curls no veil
to protect the blush on my face
of my maiden shame. In the bacchanal
chant for the dead, I come as a
celebrant, having thrown off my
veil, my bright saffron robe hanging

loose. Bring on the dead! Polynices, man of many feuds, was
well named. O woe. But your feud
was more than strife. It was murder   1590
that brought this end in blood
to the house of Oedipus. On
what bard can I call? What singer
of dirges will come now to wail
my lament? O house, my house!
As I bring these three kindred
bodies home, of a mother and her sons,
the Fury gloats at our woes
who brought this house to ruin
when my father figured out   1600
the riddle of the Sphinx,
and slew the monster.

Woe to us, father!
Your griefs are singular!
What Greek, or alien, sprung
from a high-born line,
whose lifetime race is won,
in the sight of our sun
has endured such
bitter stunning pain?   1610

On whom shall I make lamentation
and shed my shorn-off hair?
Shall I make obsequies
to the twin breasts of the
mother who nursed me? Or
on the wounds of my brothers
so cruelly slain?
Come from your chambers, blind one,
bare your sorrows ancient, who
darkened his eyes with blood   1620

so long ago. Hear me!
Your feet in gloom walk
these halls. No night
can darken you further,
groping, sightless.
(Enter Oedipus.)

OEDIPUS

Why have you drawn me to the light of day?
My hand is sightless as I searched for yours
when, from my bed, chambered with night,
I was drawn here by your lamentations—
a white-haired corpse, ghost from the   1630
underworld, living with nightmares.

ANTIGONE

I have terrible news for you, father.
Your sons are dead, and your wife,
who was the guide of your blind legs,
also is no more. O father, woe.

OEDIPUS

I can't weep and moan enough.
By what doom have these three
spirits flown from the light of life?
Tell me, child.

ANTIGONE

I speak in anguish, not with   1640
reproach or mockery. Your curse
on your sons was fulfilled
as the vengeance of hell.

OEDIPUS

Alas!

ANTIGONE
>   Why do you sigh?

OEDIPUS
>   For my boys.

ANTIGONE
>   Grief is an agony.
>   If you could take
>   the sun-god's chariot
>   to cast your glances down   1650
>   on these three corpses.

OEDIPUS
>   The evil fate of my sons,
>   brothers at war, I
>   understand. But my wife,
>   once happy, so unhappy?
>   Why was she slain?

ANTIGONE
>   She died in tears and lamentations.
>   She came a suppliant to her sons
>   to have them cease their quarrel
>   of spears wielded at one another   1660
>   like the paws of wild lions.
>   In a flowering meadow beside
>   Electra's gate she found them
>   at swordpoints, wounded, their
>   blood already spilled that would
>   shortly leave them still and cold,
>   Hades' blessing, given her by Ares,
>   and when she saw such carnage
>   Jocasta snatched a hammered bronze
>   blade from the murdered boys and thrust   1670
>   it through her neck, out of grief

for her offspring, whom she clasped
in her arms as she died in the dust.
The marshaled griefs of our line
are so terrible to behold, as they
gather against our house today.
It's the work of god . . .

CHORUS

After so much ill to Oedipus' house,
can a happier life be yet to come?

CREON

Enough lamentations. It's time we   1680
attended to burial. Hear me, Oedipus.
Your son Eteocles made me sovereign
of this city, a marriage dower to my
son Haemon's union with Antigone.
Therefore I decree you cannot live here
any longer, for as Tiresias plainly said,
Thebes shall never prosper while you
dwell inside the city. Go forth
immediately, I say, not as your enemy,
but fearing harm to Thebes because   1690
you're cursed and linger here . . .

OEDIPUS

From the start Fate bred me wretchedly,
with pain beyond all other men endure
even as I came to light outside the womb.
Phoebus warned Laius when I was just his wish
that I would someday be my father's murderer,
and, startled by my quickening breath, my father
saw me and cast me from his house, declaring
I should die, a suckling, wretched prey
to beasts . . . But I was saved!   1700

If only Cithaeron had plunged to the
bottomless chasms of the underworld
for not destroying me, but you gave me
a different Fate, as bondman to Polybus,
my lord. So ill-fated, I met Laius and
I killed my father, wenched with mother
in her bed, and begat these two brothers,
whom I have now killed, bequeathing
Laius' curse to them. I was not born
so witless as to devise these ruins   1710
for my eyes and kill my sons, but
god devised it for me with his hand.
How to dispose of such a wretched self!
Who will guide me in my darkness?
She who is dead? If she were still
alive I know she would. My two good sons?
They're also blind in death. Am I too feeble
to support myself? How? Kill me now, Creon,
for casting me from Thebes is killing me.
I will not grasp your knees as cowards do;   1720
undone I won't betray my noble roots.

CREON

It's good you do not grasp my knees to plead.
I cannot let you stay within this city.
Now let us bear Eteocles through our halls.
His brother, who came here to sack our Thebes,
must lie unearthed beyond our borders.
And this I shall proclaim to all the Thebans:
"Whoever wreaths this corpse,
or hides the body in a grave beneath
our soil, shall find reward in death.   1730
Unmourned, unburied Polynices shall be
meat for carrion birds." As for you, Antigone,
leave us, and go indoors, and protect your maidenhood
until tomorrow when Haemon's marriage bed awaits you.

ANTIGONE

Father, what misery afflicts us now?
More than the dead I mourn for you.
Your grief is not mixed up with other
feelings; in misery you're purified.
Uncle, our new king, I question you:
Why banish this man from his place of birth?   1740
And why make laws about my brother's corpse?

CREON

This edict was Eteocles', not mine.

ANTIGONE

Enforcing it is stupid.

CREON

Should I not do as I was once commanded?

ANTIGONE

Not if the doing's wrong.

CREON

Is it not right to cast him to the dogs?

ANTIGONE

This vengeance goes beyond the law.

CREON

His act was treasonous. He was born a Theban.

ANTIGONE

Has he not paid for that with his life?

CREON

And he must forfeit burial as well.   1750

ANTIGONE

What was his sin? He came to claim his throne.

CREON

And he shall have no burial, be assured.

ANTIGONE

If the State won't bury him I will.

CREON

If you do that you'll die and be buried too.

ANTIGONE

How glorious to lie beside his body.

CREON

Seize the girl, and haul her within the palace!

ANTIGONE

Never! I'll not abandon him.

CREON

The gods know better, girl, than you.

ANTIGONE

And they've decreed: do not outrage the dead!

CREON

None shall spread damp earth across this body.   1760

ANTIGONE

Do it for his mother's sake, Jocasta's . . .

CREON

Your words will not convince me.

ANTIGONE
Let me at least wash my brother's body.

CREON
This also is forbidden by the State.

ANTIGONE
His cruel wounds should be bandaged.

CREON
In no way shall you honor him in death.

ANTIGONE *(bending over the body)*
Then I will kiss you on the lips farewell, beloved.

CREON
Do not mar your nuptials with such lamentation.

ANTIGONE
Do you think that I'll still marry Haemon?

CREON
You must! Where will you take refuge from his bed?   1770

ANTIGONE
As Danaus' daughters slew those whom they
wed, so I will comport myself . . .

CREON *(to Oedipus)*
Listen to her railing in her recklessness.

ANTIGONE *(raising her brother's sword)*
Witness this sword by which I swear.

CREON
Why be so eager to avoid your bridal joy?

ANTIGONE

I will share exile with my unhappy father.

CREON

A noble gesture, though full of folly.

ANTIGONE

And with him I will end my life. Know this, uncle.

CREON

Go. Leave the land. Rather that than kill my son.
(He exits.)

OEDIPUS

I thank you for your devotion, child.   1780

ANTIGONE

How could I marry and see you sent in exile?

OEDIPUS

Stay here in Thebes. Be happy!
I will bear my sorrows.

ANTIGONE

Who will guide you in your blindness, father?

OEDIPUS

Where Fate guides me, there will I fall and lie.

ANTIGONE

Oedipus, the riddle-solver, where is he now?

OEDIPUS

Lost! One day blessed by fate and by that same
fate ruined.

ANTIGONE
Should I not share this exile with you?

OEDIPUS
In disgrace? In exile? With a blind man?   1790

ANTIGONE
For a dutiful daughter it would be no disgrace.
It's an honor.

OEDIPUS
So I might touch your mother again,
now lead me on.

ANTIGONE *(bending with him)*
Touch her with your hand—so old, so dear!

OEDIPUS
O most helpless helpmate—mother!

ANTIGONE
Having suffered all, she lies here . . .

OEDIPUS
Eteocles and Polynices—where do they lie?

ANTIGONE
Here, side by side, outstretched.

OEDIPUS
Lay my blind hand upon their faces.   1800

ANTIGONE
There! Touch your dead children with your hand.

OEDIPUS

Dead sons, as luckless as your father.

ANTIGONE

Name most dear to me, Polynices.

OEDIPUS

Now I must tell you of another prophecy.

ANTIGONE

What now! New ills beside the old?

OEDIPUS

This wanderer is doomed to die in Athens.

ANTIGONE

What Athenian fort will shelter you?

OEDIPUS

In Colonus where the horse god lives,
Poseidon. Come now. Assist me on my trek
if you are so determined to share banishment.   1810

ANTIGONE

Exile takes us,
old man and his child.
As we leave the city
I grasp your hand
to lead you as the breeze
blows a galley
over the waves.

OEDIPUS

I'm coming, child.
Oh, lead me on.

ANTIGONE

> Most wretched of   1820
> all the girls of Thebes,
> I leave with you.

OEDIPUS

> Where shall I put my old feet?
> Daughter, hand me my staff!

ANTIGONE

> Forward, this way, with me,
> father. Let your feet follow
> my hand as in a dream.

OEDIPUS

> You who would drive
> an old man into exile—
> what terrible suffering!   1830

ANTIGONE

> Why speak of your suffering?
> Justice despises sinners,
> and can never reward folly.

OEDIPUS

> Once I reached the heights of song
> and when I solved the riddle of
> the Maid of Death, I was no fool then.

ANTIGONE

> Don't look back on the Sphinx, our shame.
> It's too late now to bask in ancient glory.
> Pitiful tears await you in exile, and
> suffering and finally death.   1840
>
> And I leave tears for all the girls
> of Thebes who were my friends, leaving
> my home with you for exiled wandering.

OEDIPUS

> You have an honest heart, alas!

ANTIGONE

> Caught up in my father's sad renown
> only exile can adorn my crown.
> I mourn the wrongs, and those done to
> my brother who leaves this palace,
> a corpse without a grave. Father,
> if it's decreed that I must die,   1850
> I'll bury Polynices in the earth.

OEDIPUS

> Look once more on your friends.

ANTIGONE

> Why are they weeping? My own laments suffice.

OEDIPUS

> Turn and pray to the holy altars.

ANTIGONE

> The gods are weary of my tale of misery.

OEDIPUS

> Then go to the shrine of Bacchus in the hills,
> where only Maenads are welcome.

ANTIGONE

> To render homage without heart
> to that god to whom I once went
> in Theban fawnskins, dancing   1860
> my part in Semele's holy ritual,
> would be a profanation.

OEDIPUS

> People of Thebes, hear me, I am Oedipus,
> who read the riddle of the Sphinx,
> formerly a man of great estate,
> whose prowess quelled her murderous
> rampage. It's I who go now dishonored
> from this city into piteous exile.
> To lament these things and mourn
> for them is vain. We're doomed to errors   1870
> that the gods through Fate constrain.

(Antigone and Oedipus exit.)

CHORUS

> Hail Victory!
> Protect the crown!

Iphigenia at Aulis

Translated by
Elaine Terranova

A young woman, firstborn, mother's helper, the minder of babies, her father's favorite. What has she to look forward to? The chorus describes it: "a calm bed," a quiet happiness. Marriage to a man of her class. A new home, though it might be in a far province. Children of her own. A life that asks of her only what she has been carefully prepared for. So modest, pure, obedient, could she lose her way, give herself to a stranger as Helen, her aunt, has done? Could she too become a "destroyer of cities"?

Ancient Greece. A place, a time when people are on a first-name basis with gods, rivers, trees. So at home in the world. What can that world be like so much nearer its beginnings? The palace at Argos. Dark halls, walls whose thick stones might only have been stacked by a Cyclops. They surround the girl, separate her from what lies outside. Then what thin light sifts down to her on rays of sun and dust motes?

How do I imagine it? What can I hear or know of this, sitting in a cozy second floor parlor of the Sweet Briar library? The room, witty and feminine, tapered yellow candlesticks on the mantle, nearly invisible against the bright yellow walls; petit point sofas with that funny pattern of zoo animals you see when you look closely. The safe midnight walk back to the house on a moonlit path. Once, deer leap across it.

Chilly outside, but in here I melt into the subject. So much, though, is forbidding: my ignorance of classical history, the strategies of war or parts of ships. All I can latch onto is the music, the myths, and the names. The child tapped for something, for some unexpected destiny. Yellow walls, bright light. Myself closed off with the words I never actually see and don't know how to decipher but must take someone else's word for.

And E.'s sunlit studio, where this translation began, months before, the hottest week of summer. Dog days like those of the prologue. The garden, the sun, the hibiscus bush I unwittingly stunt while I am housesitting (I hope it has recovered). Here, too, the past has taken on a life of its own. My life feeds it. I had a father, I have a husband. This pile of books surrounding me, "unbreachable," a little like the walls surrounding the Greek woman. Her stance and her duty.

Iphigenia. A tentative, wavering word, like the stalk of her neck, the long neck of a fawn. I remember the night moonlight wiped out the path and a herd of half-starved deer leaped across. Light and dark, reinforcing the mechanisms of the play: intelligence and ignorance, truth and lies. The human, the animal. Iphigenia is the deer. It is her mirror image.

Artemis, the hunter-goddess, wants revenge because the army has killed her sacred animals. Iphigenia might have been picked at random like any prey. She has the same lack of consciousness or guilt, will yield at last in the same grammar of surrender. But how she makes a yes of that final no of nothingness is the point.

Sacrifice. It is better if the victim consents. It is said that the heads of sacrificial animals were sprinkled with holy water so that, shaking it off, they seemed to be nodding yes. A difference between sacrifice and murder. That way there was no guilt. And here is the girl, acquiescing in her own sacrifice.

Translation? Ancient Greek? The series editor encouraged me to try 100 lines. "You will know this play better than any you have seen or read. Almost as well as if you had written it." I spent a long time sitting on my hands. I am no scholar: *hubris* was a Greek word I knew. How to make sense of this rich, lost world, these improbable events? Should I care about these people? There was a hopeless pathos in the action of the play that made me uncomfortable. Infanticide. Human sacrifice. Martyrdom. The father agreeing to kill his daughter. The daughter convinced in the end to offer herself, to turn against herself, for the sake of Greece. Could I empathize? Did Euripides want me to? One hundred lines. Then I could shut the book. Like counseling an infant to take 100 steps and stop if she didn't like it; she'd never have to walk again. In the end, I did try and didn't stop.

Translation. Is it so different in itself from the first writing? A process: from other versions into my own poetry. A step away from a poem that happens in my head as well as two steps from the original play. The human essence of the thing, like the log in the fire, transmuted into another form. My starting point is the Loeb Library, so that I must translate the Victorian idiom of A. S. Way, sometimes as opaque to me as the Greek, which I do not understand at all.

I wanted to find an appropriate level of diction—like a pitch in music, one Euripides might have used and with which I could try to harmonize. Up and down the stairs I carried my (hardback) Roget's, a dictionary, a classical encyclopedia, and the published translations I was looking at to explain to myself the Loeb. I sifted through stacks of words, "unvexed: un-hindered, not held back, unhampered, without delay, not routed, released; *opp.*: restrained, obstructed."

I wanted so much to make it new though sometimes I couldn't. How was I to shake the Euripides from my head, or at least the voice I imagined was his? I might have wanted the characters to speak like people in a Mamet play, but there was my own poetry to contend with as well.

A play, I knew, was sentiment put into speech, and a playwright friend reminded me, "There are things people do not need to say." So I had to think what a person would be comfortable saying or hearing said. This was not easy, given all the other imperatives. For instance, I wanted to write in verse and picked a rough iambic, going anywhere from four to seven stresses, for the dialogue and a shorter trimeter line for the choral odes. Although in a format like this there is a temptation to fill out the line for rhythm, whether the words are needed for sense or not, I tried not to give in to it.

The choral odes I recognized as lyric poetry. I related to them immedi-ately. They expressed feelings and wishes I could have written in my own poems. I saw sensuality in that first ode, not the naval catalog based on a passage in the *Iliad*. At least one translation I looked at relegates this ode to the appendix because it delays the action of the play. But I thought of it as part of the action. I wanted to cultivate the women's role in the proceedings. More than a war between Greece and Troy (the army has not yet left to fight) Aulis is the domestic shore of the conflict—here it is a domestic war. The differences lie between father and mother, patriarchal and matriarchal authority, men and women. The second ode even more obviously repre-sents the sentiments of women. It contrasts calm, married love with the heat and lightning of Helen's elopement. The women of Calchis, perhaps with a sigh, advocate the choice they have made.

My first sense of the chorus, those bystanders from Calchis, is that they must be camp followers. What other women would turn up here? But the few classical scholars I confided this thought to pointed out that Euripides created the chorus as a reflection of the audience, decent, right-minded, middle-class. Their voluptuous enjoyment of the half-nude troops and preoccupation with Helen's love life of course didn't disqualify them as "honest" women. It would be the spectacle that drew them, accompanied by their husbands, the way tourists are drawn to Annapolis for a day trip. Think only of the ordinariness of their lives. This is a day, as they say, they won't forget. And they are needed to contrast with the House of Atreus, highborn people tottering on the edge. They are here for the sake of the audience, to evaluate the action and provide objective commentary. "Young woman," they reassure Iphigenia, "this is not your doing. Fate and the goddess are to blame."

Iphigenia has been raised at her mother's side, caring for younger siblings. Why does she suddenly switch from begging for her life to insisting on her death? Is it a simple acceptance of the writing on the wall, or has she looked past her situation to a greater glory—the kind a man gains when he gives up his life to a cause he believes in? I think Euripides is telling us that war is a mistake. It could be prevented if leaders were not self-serving and fighting men didn't lust for adventure and blood. Iphigenia, then, may be tragically mistaken, but she is caught up in the patriarchal dream of glory. She gives up marriage, home, and children, those signposts of female virtue, to do what her father asks of her and through him, the state. Iphigenia takes a hero's pride in her role, even if it hasn't been her idea. Yes, Odysseus is coming for her, but she chooses her fate—a woman, she is the bravest warrior of the play. And, tender-hearted though she is, she even forbids Achilles to kill in her name, she is ultimately responsible for the deaths of thousands and the destruction of Troy—Euripidean irony.

It seemed too easy to cut all the speeches from the same cloth, the serviceable, even wording of translation. I tried to differentiate among these people. I wanted each to have some personal relationship to humor, anger, despair, to contrast with everyone else. This is a thinking man's Achilles, for instance, and not the bloodthirsty demigod of the *Iliad*. "It's a terrible thing to die," he will admit here. And Clytemnestra is not yet a danger to Agamemnon, although the threat is there. She is earthy and a fighter, but she is also the good mother. For her own as well as her daughter's sake, she refuses to bow down to patriarchal authority.

The characters in this play change their minds often, as people do. Euripides models the complexity of his characters with an irony that might be mistaken for inconsistency but surely isn't. "A life spent in misery is better than the most glorious death," says Iphigenia, but 200 lines later she begs to die for Greece and be praised as if she "were immortal."

I expected this translation to be shorter than the original—I was told that ancient Greek has a tendency to shrink in English. In fact, it took me 300 more lines than it took Euripides. I added images, metaphors, connectors, even stage directions that I thought might help my version approximate the emotional range of the original. I have kept the interpolated ending believed to have been added by Euripides' son or nephew, but with an intervening dark stage after the main action of the drama.

Many people have helped in this translation. First is my editor, David Slavitt, who planted the idea for it and trusted me to accomplish it. I learned much from his example. I am grateful too for the support of my comrades-in-arms, Buffy Morgan, whose *Elektra* was taking shape at the same time and with whom I was able to share discoveries and conundrums, and Eleanor Wilner, who generously offered a workspace and the loan of reference books to help me begin and lively discussion of styles and preferences in translation. As a novice, I was glad, too, to have access to the fine translations of Moses Hadas and John McLean, Charles R. Walker, and W. S. Merwin and George E. Dimock, Jr., and to have seen Cacoyannis' film, *Iphigenia*.

Cast

AGAMEMNON, commander of the Greek army
OLD SERVANT of Agamemnon and Clytemnestra
CHORUS of women of Chalcis who have come to see the
    Greek fleet
MENELAUS, Agamemnon's brother and Helen's husband
MESSENGER
CLYTEMNESTRA, Agamemnon's wife
IPHIGENIA, daughter of Agamemnon and Clytemnestra
ACHILLES, warrior and hero
NONSPEAKING
    Attendants
    Armor bearers
    Orestes, infant son of Agamemnon and Clytemnestra

(*The harbor of Aulis where the Greek ships are at a standstill,
    waiting to sail to Troy. Agamemnon is standing in front of his
    tent; the old servant is approaching.*)

AGAMEMNON
    Where are you, old man? Come out beside my tent.

OLD SERVANT
    I'm here, master, or soon will be. What is it you want?

AGAMEMNON
    Move faster. Do you sleep on your feet?

OLD SERVANT
    Not I. I scarcely sleep. Age is a sentry
    posted at these eyes so that they don't dare close.

AGAMEMNON

> Tell me, what star is looking down at us,
> the one riding heaven's waves at this hour?

OLD SERVANT

> Sirius, the dog star, the hunter's
> companion. The dog days are chafing at our heels.

AGAMEMNON

> No wonder then, I hear no sound of life beside us,   10
> no bird call or sea breeze.
>   Aulis is still.
> The guards stand like stone pillars on the walls.

OLD SERVANT

> Yet there's no peace for you, Lord Agamemnon,
> strutting up and down before your tent,
> arush like the wind. Come, let's go inside.

AGAMEMNON

> I envy you. You live your long, safe years unnoticed.
> A man who shines above the rest is cursed.
> His brightness tempts heaven. Better to be you,
> old man, who scarcely nod your head above the earth
> like some low flower.

OLD SERVANT

>   But glory boosts you up   20
> to the heights in this life.

AGAMEMNON

>   Yes, and grasps your knees
> and pulls you to the ground. Ruin's tied to greatness.
> We infuriate the gods when we try most
> to please them. Our own fate topples us.
> So how should we prevail against other men
> who are our enemies?

OLD SERVANT
                    What is this bray of self-doubt
from the mouth of a king? You were born a man,
the seed of Atreus, Agamemnon.
Sun and darkness are meant equally to mottle
your path. You were put on this earth to serve the gods,   30
for why should they serve you?
                       But you have lit your lamp.
Is this a letter you are writing?
I see your words darkening the page,
though you have undone half of them.
First you hold the letter out to me,
then you snatch it back to hide your heart.
The seal is nearly melted by your tears.

What mad grief has taken hold of you?
Let me share this hidden sorrow. Remember,
I came to you with Clytemnestra,   40
so trustworthy that Tyndareus
picked me for your wedding train.

AGAMEMNON
                      I'll tell you, then,
but you won't thank me. I will be paying back
your loyalty in grief. Anyhow, some of it
you know: How Leda, the child of Thestius,
had three daughters: Phoebe, my wife, Clytemnestra,
and Helen. All were fair, all marriageable,
though Helen's more than mortal beauty
drew each prince of Greece. They were the fishermen
who came for such a catch. Each was so blinded   50
by her that he swore to kill the rest.
It was up to wily Tyndareus
to keep them from slaughtering one another
so there was no one left to take the girl,
or turning on himself. He made them join

their right hands in a pledge and seal it
with burnt offerings and poured-out wine.
Let Helen choose, and if anyone, Greek or barbarian,
should dispossess that man from her bed, they'd braid
their loyalty and might avenging him,   60
razing the walls of the usurper's town and house
to win her back. So Tyndareus outsmarted them
and let his daughter safely take her pick.

Then, was it a sigh, or a scent on the wind
that turned her head to Menelaus?
Oh, anyone but him! For he let Paris in,
who once judged Aphrodite lovelier
than her sister goddesses. Paris,
who, in foreign, gold-embroidered robes,
disguised himself to Menelaus as a friend,   70

entering his house. Great fool! Helen saw
and loved the man and ran off with him
to his ranch lands on Mt. Ida. Menelaus
whirled through Greece, stung by rage to madness.
He claimed the aid of everyone who swore the oath,
convincing them his shame spilled over onto them.
The suitors sprang up in clanging mail, clasping weapons.
They anchored their shining ships beside his
within the narrow straits of Aulis.
For Menelaus' sake, because I am his brother,   80
they named me captain of the host.
Oh, woeful honor I would part with happily!

And so we stood, united, to sack Troy.
But a dead calm chained the sea and held us here.
In our despair because we could not sail
we listened to the prophet Calchas, who rose up,
claiming he spoke for heaven. Artemis, he said,
the maiden goddess who rules this place,

required from us the sacrifice of a maiden.
As I was chief, it must be my daughter,   90
my first-born, Iphigenia. This carnage,
Calchas swore, would free our ships and bring us
victory, but if we did not slay the girl
our enterprise would fail. In my horror
I ordered Talthybius to blast his trumpet
and disband the host. How could I kill my child?

But my brother wheedled and begged me,
for honor's sake, for our very lives,
since the army might turn on us without her blood.
At last I was persuaded. The girl must come,   100
although to lure her, I made the purpose love,
not death. A marriage with Achilles,
bragging of his greatness and his love for her.
A ruse, and yet it rinsed the evil from my mind,
myself half-imagining a future.
I told her he would not sail without a bride
to cheer his empty halls in Phthia.
So many false assurances. I made them,
I suppose, for Clytemnestra's sake.
The hoax was mine. No one knew of it   110
but Calchas, Odysseus, and Menelaus.

If I can still undo what has been done,
lift that shadow from my soul—you saw me
break the letter's seal. Now only truth,
bright truth is captured here. Until you reach Argos,
let the words lie hidden in your heart and hand.
Trusted slave, so many years you've proved yourself
loyal to my wife and house.

OLD SERVANT

                              I will do
all you ask, and be as true to the words you speak,
as to those written in your hand.   120

AGAMEMNON
  Then you shall know them.
(*reads*)

                              "Clytemnestra, Leda's child,
  I was too hasty. Iphigenia
  must not come. The wind we wait for never blows.
  The tide is fastened to Euboea's rocky shore.
  Let us put off the wedding for a better time,
  when the rites are sanctioned by good weather
  and the ships can sail."

OLD SERVANT
                      And the bride that's promised
  to Achilles? Anger will swell up in his breast
  like a storm. He will rage against you and your wife.
  Surely, this is a perilous course.   130

AGAMEMNON
  Achilles never lent his name to my deceit.
  He is as blameless as the maiden. It's only I
  who offer his arms to her in a husband's embrace.

OLD SERVANT
  Oh, fear what you have done. You will answer for it—
  making a death offering of the bride
  you name for him. Achilles is a goddess' son.

AGAMEMNON
  You are right, old man. I'm lost. The world is spinning,
  hurling me to my ruin. Go quickly. Go!
  Age no more in your mission.

OLD SERVANT
                      Nothing
  will hold me back, my lord.

AGAMEMNON

Don't stop to eat   140
or drink. And though you may thirst for it more,
don't for a moment taste sleep.

OLD SERVANT

Never doubt me.

AGAMEMNON

Let your eyes search each fork in the road
for my daughter's chariot, rolling to where
the dry land stops and the ships wait.
Don't let anything that moves pass you.
And when you come across her, grab the horses' reins
to halt the train if you have to. Send her back
to Mycenae, safe behind the Cyclops' wall,
that watchful citadel she came from.   150
Through these gates, now. Hurry on your way!

OLD SERVANT

I will do what you command.

But how
should your wife and daughter know what to believe?
You have called them to Aulis for the wedding feast.

AGAMEMNON

Show them this seal and its imprint, where it
pressed the letter, like my lips. Go now. Save me.
You must. Lift me from this pit of my own making.
Ah, no one's luck will hold from first to last.
Each day we draw our lots for happiness
while fortune looks the other way.   160

(Exit Agamemnon and servant. Enter Chorus of women of Chalcis.)

CHORUS
>   I have come in a small boat
>   through the mighty waters of the Euripus,
>   from Chalcis, my home. My city stands
>   at the opening to the sea,
>   suckling that bright fountain, Arethusa.
>
>   I came to see the armies in battle raiment
>   and the Greek armada,
>   cresting like a golden wave
>   on the shore. The thousand ships,
>   with their host of heroes, dazzled me.   170
>   They make their war for love, I know.
>   Bright-haired Menelaus summoned them.
>   Beside him, Agamemnon stands,
>   his brother and support,
>   Menelaus who lost his wife to smiling Paris.
>
>   The goddess of love herself
>   gave Helen to the Trojan,
>   Aphrodite, still dewy from her forest bath,
>   when Paris chose her beauty
>   over Hera's or Athena's. As a reward   180
>   he took the wife of Menelaus
>   and brought her to the waving grasslands
>   of his kingdom.
>
>   Burnt offerings lined my path
>   as I came to the groves of Artemis.
>   A good wife I was, and shy,
>   approaching the campground.
>   There I saw warriors
>   emerging from their tents,
>   bare-legged and strong, in simple tunics.   190
>   Blushes dyed my cheeks.

I watched the sweating horses,
team after team of the chariots,
run through their paces.

Someone pointed out the two Ajaxes,
one, the son of Oileus, the other,
of Telamon, the Crown Prince of Salamis.
I saw Protesilaus
and Poseidon's Palamedes
joking as they sat at each side   200
of a game board, confounding
one another with their moves. Diomedes,
with heart-soaring joy, threw the discus.
And all of us marveled at Meriones,
in gold armor, so like his war-god father.
And I gazed for a long while
at the best looking of the Achaeans,
Laertes' son, shining through the sea mist,
and Nireus, even handsomer.

I saw Achilles run.   210
His feet are fast as horses' hooves,
as fast as storm winds.
He raced a chariot and four
along the hard-packed sand.
Dappled gray thoroughbreds,
plumed and gold-bridled, shared the yoke;
two bays with spotted fetlocks flanked them.
Lap after lap, they swept the course,
while Achilles, gold-armored,
kept pace with the carriage wheels.   220
At each turn, the charioteer, Eumelus,
whipped the hard-breathing horses
till their mouths lathered
and their hides were flecked
with a snow of whiteness, urging them on.

Then I came to where the vessels lie.
I am a woman. What do I know
of ships and the parts of ships?
Yet I marveled. Wave after wave,
an ocean of ships, rolling on.   230
And oh, the heart swell of pride
as I greeted them, their might,
their promise of conquest.
Fifty fast galleys from Phthia
made up the whole right wing,
each bearing gold idols of the Nereids,
Achilles' protectors, nymphs related to his mother.
Nearby lay ships of other famed Argives
and of the young and untried, too,
who come with their fathers' blessings,   240
shining with the brightness of that old glory
and the hope pinned on themselves.
Each vessel carries idols and signs
of the family gods watching over them.

I saw the fifty craft of Mecistes' boy.
Beside him stood Sthenelus,
whose father is Capaneus.
Battle station after battle station
is manned by heroes and heroes' sons,
even the heir of Theseus,   250
with another fifty sleek ships.
The sun's car blazed on their bulwarks,
Athena at the reins of winged horses,
to make the oarsmen fly.

Anchored in shallow water beside shore
was Boeotia's navy,
led by Leitus, a son of Earth.
The likeness of Cadmus appeared on each galley
and the gold dragon whose teeth he sowed

to harvest warriors.   260
Afterward came ships from Phocis,
captained by Oileus' son.
Stories abound of his home, Thronium.

And here were the sons of Atreus
from the Titans' palace of Mycenae.
Menelaus, himself,
cuckolded by the foreign prince,
who enlisted these golden warriors of Greece
to ravish Troy and drag away his wife.
His friend and brother, Agamemnon,   270
commands their hundred ships,
no force too large, lodged as they are
at the eye of the storm.
And farther, the river Alpheus,
depicted as a bull, looked down
from the prows of Gerenian Nestor,
king of Pylos, the sacred river's source.

Then came twelve galleys of the Aenians,
led by king Gouneus,
and after them, the chiefs of Elis,   280
known as Epeians.
Eurytus was captain of their fleet.
He led the Taphians too,
and whether their galleys were called
white-oared for the speed of the rowers,
or because they were fashioned of pure silver,
I do not know.
It is said the rocky ravages of their home,
the Echinead Isles,
beached many a sailor for all time.   290

Ajax, foster child of Salamis,
joined the navy's left wing to the right,

with twelve stout battleships
flexed between them
like the backbone of a giant bird.

Oh, what a spectacle glinting on sea and shore,
vast warbird, vast engine
that carries glorious warriors
off to conquer or to die!
I will lay myself before you.   300
I will keep you in my heart.
(Enter old servant, struggling with Menelaus.)

OLD SERVANT

Give me back my letter, Menelaus.
Don't shame yourself as well as me.
This is not your business.

MENELAUS

Is it yours?
Loyalty chains you to your master's house.

OLD SERVANT

That fault others might consider a virtue.

MENELAUS

Go any further and you will risk annoying me.

OLD SERVANT

You have no right to break the wax seal,
or the more binding one, of privacy.

MENELAUS

And who gave you the right to compromise   310
us all and wreck the Greek alliance?

OLD SERVANT

That choice belongs to one more great than I.
Let me have my letter and be gone.

MENELAUS

The matter is in my hands now.

OLD SERVANT

                              Not yet.
I am holding onto it and will not let go.

MENELAUS

Your will is self-delusion, slave. I am king.
Soon I'll bloody your head with my scepter.

OLD SERVANT

Then I will die with honor for my master's sake.
(Enter Agamemnon.)
Lord Agamemnon, he is overpowering me.
He has torn your letter out of my hands.   320
He has no regard for what's right.

AGAMEMNON

What is this commotion at my door?

MENELAUS

Schemer! I broke that seal to know what lay behind it.

AGAMEMNON

What am I guilty of then? You find a scheme
where you look for it, in the mud, to darken my name.

MENELAUS

I know you sent the old man to turn
your daughter back to Argos.

AGAMEMNON

Don't overstep yourself.
On whose authority do you dare
interfere in my affairs?

MENELAUS

On my own authority.
I am not your slave.

AGAMEMNON

Not my master, either.   330
Where did you waylay my servant?

MENELAUS

Nothing of the kind. He approached,
with his shambling, old man's gait, as I waited
outside the camp for Iphigenia
and our deliverance.

AGAMEMNON

That's my concern.
You have no say in it.

MENELAUS

Oh, I'm central to it.

AGAMEMNON

Are you contradicting me? I wield
the rod in my own house.

MENELAUS

Hah! A poor, thin stick it is,
It twists in the wind, putting down no roots
in loyalty.

AGAMEMNON

            Glib words. You sniff out   340
evil everywhere. I distrust your thoughts.
They slide too easily to your tongue.

MENELAUS

I tell you, be careful, Agamemnon.
The heart that heaves with betrayal is a hornet's nest.
You're poison to your friends. I tell you
for your own sake. Let the truth prick you,
swollen as you are with pride and honor.
It was not the wrong done to me but your own wish
that made you warlord. That view, the whole armada
with you at its center, with god-grace   350
and auspicious winds, rowing toward Troy.
Outwardly, you shrank from ambition,
but your right hand claimed the right hand
of anyone who passed by. The doors of your palace
were open to any grievance. You wooed, you begged
like a would-be bridegroom. You put a name
to each man's face, high and low. Soon all sought you.
Outdoors, you minced and let them hail you.
Oh, what was the market price of your good will?
Surely, your great popularity   360
won you the command. Then suddenly you were like
the sun in eclipse. Your face darkened.
Who knew, looking at you, if they were friend to you
or foe? You shut your door to everyone:
out of sight, out of reach. You were exalted,
wreathed in clouds. You might have raised up others—
that's what good fortune demands. You had your fill.
Then let prosperity spill over
into the laps of your friends. I blame you
for this and more, much more.

                             You brought   370
the Greek forces to Aulis, though here

no favorable wind was waiting to dispatch them.
An evil spell turned them to statues,
until the separate kings begged to disband them.
Then you looked bewildered. Master of a thousand ships,
godlike, yet you could not think how to release
that rain of spears on Priam's beach.
What should be said of you? Not the greatness
you dreamed of to sing you down through posterity.
Contempt rather: "He made war but no one came."   380
Then you turned to me for help, so that
you'd keep your rank and the glory that clung to it.
And when Calchas came to you with the sign
from Artemis, to lay your daughter
like a helpless hind on the altar, "Is that all?"
you asked. "Is that all it takes to free
my ships?" That easily you promised your child
to the slaying stone, of your free will, your own
design. You sent for her, hailed Clytemnestra
mother of the bride, gulling both with the picture   390
of Achilles' waiting arms. The heavens heard you then
and hear you now, saying that Iphigenia
will not die. You lie to man and god alike,
whatever whim takes you. And you are not the first.
Perhaps the air is thinner where you are.
How many like you, high and mighty,
fall to the depths of self-delusion?
Those they rule they think are shadows of themselves,
desiring what they desire. The populace,
I tell you, is a separate animal.   400
Shrewdness is needed to tame it. I feel for Greece.
Where is her triumph, great beast, when she
is held in check for you and your daughter's sake?

Let me never put kinship first! Though you
are my brother, I see you cannot rule
yourself, much less the whole Greek host.

CHORUS
> Here are two mirror images, mouthing strife,
> though each came to daylight from the same womb.

AGAMEMNON
> Now, brother to brother, it's my turn.
> No high-blown sentiments from me. Despite   410
> what you say, I keep the earth in sight.
>
> Yes, rage, rage. There's blood in your eye
> and fire on your breath. What can be wrong?
> What do you lack that I, your brother, can supply?
> A faithful wife? I'm no magician, man.
> You let the one you had out of your grasp.
> You could no more hold on to her than to
> the feathered god who fathered her. Whereas
> I rule my womenfolk. I shape them to my will.
> It must be envy then that seeds your words.   420
> Do you wish the Greeks had made you their chief?
> More likely, though, it's lust that tortures you,
> the empty bed, the randy goat's bleat on your lips.

(Menelaus tries to interfere.)

> No. Don't silence me. Your bloodshot eyes,
> your face puffed up like an adder. But you have no sting.
> A fountain of wisdom, your advice?
> This stagnant pool, splashing mud up into my face?
> Listen to me. You are without her now?
> The gods have only corrected your mistake.
> A wind blew Helen to you once and then   430
> blew her away. The stench of evil's left your house.
> Be glad of it. I made an error, too.
> I am undoing it. Your loss? I cannot
> make it up to you by slaughtering my children.
> What—put a virgin to death to free a whore?
> If I took a sword to my first-born, tear for tear,
> I'd match each drop of blood. There'd be no space

in night or day for life continuing,
sunlight only crashing through my reveries.

Let the suitors flock to you. Your misery   440
is their magnet. Marriage-crazed, you and the others
swore to bring Helen back. Together, then,
make your war. I break the promise forced on me.
It would be mad to honor it.

CHORUS
                              These new words
    sweep away the old. But yes! Far better
    to protect the child.

MENELAUS
                    I see I have no friends.

AGAMEMNON
    Those you wish harm won't stay your friends for long.

MENELAUS
    Lost too, that brother-bond I thought I could depend on.
    Are you still our father's son?

AGAMEMNON
                              In his wisdom I am.
    Not in the blood heat of child slaughter.   450

MENELAUS
    If you were my brother and my friend, you would
    know my pain.

AGAMEMNON
                    Have you suddenly
    befriended me? Good. Then swallow your words.
    Keep that venom in your soul in check.

MENELAUS

                Yes. Given the chance,
he'd overstep himself, rise up and rule.

AGAMEMNON

He was a party to the oracle.
What stops him from broadcasting Calchas' prophecy?
He will say I promised Artemis her virgin
and now leave the slaying stone bare.
What wouldn't he do to fell the tree and,   600
in the process, pluck the fruit? He'll lead them
as far as Argos in pursuit. No matter
those Cyclopean walls, the thickness of that stone.
He will see that nothing stands between us
and our fate. It's all the same to him, raze the walls
of Argos or of Troy.
(aside)

              O gods, gods.
Is there no place I can turn that you don't lie in wait,
my sworn enemies?
(to Menelaus)

              Please, brother. One favor.
Though word spreads through the camp, take care, for my sake,
that Clytemnestra hears nothing   610
until the bargain's sealed and our child
is handed over to the priests. At least that way
I'll spare us both her tears. They'd melt my will.
And you, foreign ladies, understand as well,
you must give nothing of this away.
(Exit Agamemnon and Menelaus.)

CHORUS LEADER

Let love come, a slow dance
like the sea's at low tide,
no headlong rush.
A time of quiet meeting,

of bowing to one another and waiting,   620
orderly, agreeable. Not fever,
all-consuming, but slow kindling.
An awakening, the body's slow stretch,
inch by inch, toward feeling.
I am thinking of the two strands
of Eros' bow. Oh, let the arrow
be struck off the one foretelling
tender bliss, not the other,
though its double,
which guarantees unrest.   630

SECOND VOICE
Aphrodite, never let me smart
from a wound that draws me
out of a calm bed into star-fired night.
Goddess, in my desires,
let me keep a modest heat,
not turn from my lawful mate,
resist the unaccounted-for embrace
for the mild but steady light.

THIRD VOICE
We are made of marbled stone,
shot through with goodness.   640
The vein is strengthened
with each battle of the soul.
Wisdom is right-thinking, decency.
Yet for men there is no setting out
that won't have glory as its goal,
no greater lesson learned.
It is their nature and their nurturing
to take command.
Not one alone but many together
raise up the walls of cities   650

OLD SERVANT *(calling through the open door)*
>Please, both of you, stay. Don't go any farther,
>grandson of Aeacus, as much god as man,
>and you, my lady, Leda's daughter.

ACHILLES
>What voice is this that reaches me through   1010
>half-opened doors? It trembles with uncertainty.

OLD SERVANT
>It is a slave's voice, all that it can be
>in this life. That is my fortune, or misfortune.
>Maybe you hear terror in it, for I do not know
>if it has the power to influence events.

ACHILLES
>You are no slave of mine. I know them, and they
>are kept in my camp, separate from Agamemnon's.

OLD SERVANT
>I belong to the lady standing here.
>I was a gift from her father, Tyndareus,
>on the day she married Agamemnon.   1020

ACHILLES *(impatient)*
>Fine. I am glad to hear it. And now
>tell me why you've stopped me.

OLD SERVANT *(looking around)*
>   Are we alone
>here at the gates?

ACHILLES
>   We're alone. Come out
>from the king's chambers if you have something to say.

OLD SERVANT *(appearing)*
    I do. And may fate and my foresight still save
    those I wish to save.

ACHILLES *(mocking)*
                    That should give us
        hope for the future.
(Old servant bends before Clytemnestra.)

CLYTEMNESTRA
                    Don't kneel to me now.
        Say what you have come to say. Don't waste time.

OLD SERVANT
        You know me, my lady, how devoted
        I've been to you and yours?

CLYTEMNESTRA
                        I know you are loyal   1030
        and an old servant of my house.

OLD SERVANT
                    And that I was
        claimed by Agamemnon as part of your dowry?

CLYTEMNESTRA
        Yes. You came with me all those years ago
        to Argos and are with me still.

OLD SERVANT
                        So you see,
        my devotion lies with you and your children,
        over your husband.

CLYTEMNESTRA
                    Then tell me what you know.
        What are you keeping from me?

OLD SERVANT *(as if looking off and seeing it happen)*
>   Soon your husband
>   will carry your daughter to the altar
>   and raise his sword to her throat.

CLYTEMNESTRA
>   What madness
>   is this? Only in your mind's eye, old man,   1040
>   can such a hideous vision take shape.

OLD SERVANT
>   A red line around the girl's white neck—a necklace
>   of her own blood.

CLYTEMNESTRA
>   Oh, now I see it too—
>   you are telling the truth. Horror, what I see,
>   Agamemnon, murder-mad!

OLD SERVANT
>   Mad only in this,
>   where you and the child are concerned. Otherwise,
>   he is acting in his own best interest.

CLYTEMNESTRA
>   What demon has entered his soul that drives him to this?

OLD SERVANT
>   The oracle Calchas read commands her slaughter
>   so the ships can sail.

CLYTEMNESTRA
>   Child, you are lost to me now,   1050
>   promised only to death!
>   *(distracted)*
>   What was it
>   you said about ships? Where should they sail?

OLD SERVANT

Why, to Troy, to reclaim Helen from the royal halls
for Menelaus' sake.

CLYTEMNESTRA

So Helen's homecoming
rests on Iphigenia's doom?

OLD SERVANT

You have it all.
Her father has pledged the child as a sacrifice
to Artemis.

CLYTEMNESTRA

Then I am doubly wronged.
To think this phantom marriage
drew me laughing from my home to such a grief!

OLD SERVANT

But what mother would not give her daughter   1060
joyfully to Achilles as his bride?

CLYTEMNESTRA

Child, I should be your protector.
Instead, I deliver you to ruin's door
and enter there myself with you.

OLD SERVANT

Mother and daughter, I pity you. For who
could do worse to those he loves than your lord?

CLYTEMNESTRA

Is there an end to this misery? What still
lies ahead?

OLD SERVANT

Lady, no grief is greater
than to outlive one's child.

CLYTEMNESTRA

> But how did you come
> to know this? Can you be sure of what you've told me?   1070

OLD SERVANT

> Agamemnon sent me to you with a new letter.

CLYTEMNESTRA

> Had he changed his mind? Or did he still want me
> to bring the child?

OLD SERVANT

> No, he forbade you
> to bring her. He was in his right mind then.

CLYTEMNESTRA

> What has become of that letter?
> Why did you not deliver it to me?

OLD SERVANT

> Because Menelaus stole it from me,
> wronging us all.

CLYTEMNESTRA

> And you, Thetis' son,
> have you been listening to this catalogue
> of evil? They have made you an accomplice   1080
> in my daughter's death.

ACHILLES

> Oh, unwillingly!
> And now, how can I bear your suffering,
> knowing the part I've played in it?

CLYTEMNESTRA

> Truly, you were the lure that drew us here,
> that false promise of a marriage. You,

above all others, were the husband
I wanted for her.

ACHILLES

                    Then you must see
that I, too, have been wronged. Agamemnon used me,
blackening my name. I won't allow it!

CLYTEMNESTRA *(sinking to her knees)*
I feel no shame kneeling before you.   1090
Your mother was a goddess. I am only
a mortal woman, but I too have a child.
Pride will not keep me from clinging to your knees
though I am queen. My crown is my daughter—
her life gives the value to mine. I beg you,
goddess-born, I put her happiness and mine
in your hands. Protect us. She was not your bride,
except in cruel pretense, yet think of her that way.
She has no one. See how her father is willing
to crush her for his own ends. And I myself,   1100
unwittingly, have wreathed her in flowers
and led her to her slaughter.
                            Your name has been soiled.
Act bravely. Cleanse it. I beg you, by the beard
that makes you a man, by the strength in your right hand,
by your mother's divine spirit. I have no friends,
no altar but your knees. I am surrounded
by bloodthirsty adventurers in this place.
But even they have hearts. If you can bring their strength
to our side, we may still be safe. If not,
my daughter's life is lost. Do you dare, then,   1110
to hold out your hand over our heads?

CHORUS LEADER
Motherhood is fierce magic. It casts a spell
over a woman, so she will stop at nothing
to save her child.

ACHILLES

                     Lady, your grief overwhelms me.
I pity you.
(to himself)

             Yet here I am not king.
Pride can coax a fire in me—I mustn't be
too quick to act. Let me think. My tutor, Chiron,
taught me temperance. Then I will be guided
by the sons of Atreus—where they are right.
Otherwise, whether here or afterward in Troy,   1120
why should I follow them? I am a free man.
I draw my sword only to bring honor
on myself and Ares' name.
(speaking to Clytemnestra)

                   Unfortunate lady,
you find a savage cruelty in the arms
where you should most expect devotion. I am young
and haven't Agamemnon's worldly power,
but my compassion is a shield I buckle
around you. You will be saved. Your daughter
cannot die so unnaturally,
at her father's hand, nor will I let my name   1130
be the blade he holds at her throat. No!
I won't be his dupe, tainted with the blood
of an innocent girl. Not if I were
the most unprincipled of the Greeks,
Odysseus, say, or Menelaus,
could I send her to her death with this trickery.
If my father were not Peleus but someone
low-born, contemptible—then I might lend
my name to your husband's butchery. No, never!
I swear by my grandfather, Nereus,   1140
the ocean's foster son. If the king lays a hand
on his daughter, if his fingertip grazes
so much as one fold of her dress, then Troy
is not a jewel worth conquering

but an ignorant backwater, and we needn't sail.
Calchas will pay dearly for his mistake. What is
a seer, after all? A blind archer
thought to be a god when his arrow hits.
But let him miss. Then he is brought lower
than his prey. For now, let him conjure up   1150
his barley cakes and holy water. His guesses
will not pass for truth.
             And, as you see,
no marriage has been arranged between me
and Agamemnon's daughter. There are brides enough,
some as noble, who would be glad to share
a soldier's glory. Not for the world
do I want to see your child hurt, but war
has casualties. If Agamemnon had asked me
to lend my name—I say, if he had convinced me
that the success of the enterprise depended   1160
on it, even to trapping his child,
if he had shown that trust in me, I might
have been persuaded.
             But as it stands,
I see I count for nothing in his eyes.
He treats me like the dog at his heels.
He will toss me shame as easily as the bone
of honor. And so, if they come for your daughter,
my sword will taste blood before it gets to Troy.
Calm yourself. I'll watch over her as the gods do.
I will be more like them than a mortal man.   1170

CLYTEMNESTRA
How good you are—my daughter's salvation!
as if she had really been your bride.
The air should be filled with praise for you.
You are a better man than those whose orders
you obey. Forgive me. I know the truly brave
scorn flattery. I won't have you hate me.

Enough to catch you up in our wretchedness.
My pain belongs to me. The wrench of it,
you cannot feel. But we are weak and you,
from the heights of glory, bend down to us. Pity me   1180
for calling you son. You can see why I wished it.
But know that my child's death will be a shadow
hanging over you when you do marry.

I take heart from what you've said. I see my daughter
will live if you will it. Only ask
and she will kneel at your feet herself.
She is a maiden and it would demean her,
but she will do it if you say,
that innocence and trust gazing up
into your face, beseeching. If I can plead   1190
our suit alone, I'd spare her this loss of modesty.
So little belongs to a woman in this life
but her good name, and even that bows
to necessity.

ACHILLES
                    Please, she must not kneel
to me. Keep her indoors, out of sight.
This is an army camp. Why risk the crude
speculations of the rabble? There is
so little now for fools to do but wag their tongues.
Besides, the end will be the same whether either
of you pleads or not. All that matters is to save her.   1200
I swear to you, I will die protecting her.
My life will not be spared unless hers is.

CLYTEMNESTRA
The gods protect you.

ACHILLES
                    And you. You have a role to play.

CLYTEMNESTRA

Whatever it is, tell me and I'll do it.

ACHILLES

Then try to bring your husband around.

CLYTEMNESTRA

What use is that? He's too afraid. He thinks
the army will turn on him without their victim.

ACHILLES

Reason is as convincing as fear. Plead with him.
He can't kill his child. You are his life's partner,
mother of the girl—

CLYTEMNESTRA

                  It's hopeless. Those coals are dead.   1210
But say what you want me to do.

ACHILLES

                        Persuade him.
If you can't, return to me. I'll wait.
And he may relent. Then I can come as a friend
and second his thoughts to let her live.
If you can reason with him, we gain our end
and the army will not be able
to reproach me. Try, at least. I would rather
she were spared without my interference.

CLYTEMNESTRA

No doubt. I will do what seems best to you.
But what if I have no luck with Agamemnon?   1220
You're all that stands between my daughter
and the slaying stone.

ACHILLES
                    Whatever happens,
you won't be out of my sight. Don't go looking for me.
It wouldn't do to have you running wild-eyed
through the Danaan camp. That would bring shame
to you and to your father's house. Tyndareus
doesn't deserve that. He has the respect
of all the Greeks.

CLYTEMNESTRA
                    Then I'll let you govern me.
If there are gods in heaven, they'll reward you.
If not, what point is there in anything we do?   1230
(Exit Achilles and Clytemnestra.)

CHORUS
    Oh, what was the song piped
    by a Libyan flute and echoed on the lyre,
    the one they played when Peleus,
    Aeacus' son, took Thetis as his wife?
    Oh, glad beginning!
    The gods made the feast,
    and that day brought joy to everyone.
    The Graces entered, dancing to that song,
    imprinting the earth
    with their shining sandals.   1240
    Oh, radiant dancers!

    Ganymede, Zeus' favorite,
    poured out the wine from a golden bowl.
    The guests made long and elegant toasts.
    Praise and music swept over
    woodlands and the centaurs' hills,
    announcing the marriage.
    Oh, the intoxication of music and wine!

Then, as bridesmaids,
fifty Nereids rose gleaming from the sea   1250
and wove the marriage dance along the sands.
And soon packs of centaurs rode down
like mounted horsemen.
They wore laurel wreaths and carried lances.
Oh, what do they crave above wine?
With brimming bowls, they drank
the health of Thetis.
"Sea Queen," they called,
"the light of all Thessaly
will come from your womb."   1260
And Chiron named this son Achilles,
saying, "He will lead his Myrmidons
with blazing spear and shield through Priam's land."

And that is how the gods
crowned Nereus' daughter with happiness
and brought her from her father's land
under the sea to the arms of Peleus.

LEADER

    While a wreath of death flowers
will circle Iphigenia's yellow hair.
And she will be led still innocent   1270
like a white and red heifer
down the hill, white neck running
with the blood of sacrifice.
You weren't bred for this,
to be called to slaughter
by the herder's shrill pipe.
Your mother is a queen.
She raised you at her side
to stand hand in hand with a king's son.
Then why should I cover my bosom   1280
and cast down my eyes

when men put aside decency for greed
and honor themselves above gods?
The law is trampled over
and no one agrees any longer
on what is good or holy.
(Enter Clytemnestra.)

CLYTEMNESTRA

How long will my lord keep me waiting? I won't budge
until he comes.
                    The girl's sobs still hang in the air.
I am sure they shatter the peace of anyone
who hears them, a low moan like wind through ruined trees.   1290
It began when she learned that her father
has plotted to kill her.
                    Ah, he is coming now,
as if my words drew him, bearing witness against him
for the murder of his child.

AGAMEMNON *(disguising his discomfort)*
                    Clytemnestra,
Leda's child. How lucky I am to find you.
We have matters to talk about in private,
without troubling the bride.

CLYTEMNESTRA
                    Are you saying
there are words fit for the occasion?

AGAMEMNON

Send for the girl. The holy water's poured,
and the barley is ready for sprinkling   1300
on the flames. All that's left is to dedicate
the victims to Artemis and honor her
with fresh blood.

CLYTEMNESTRA *(aside)*
                         Oh, honey drips from your mouth.
     But what is it you don't say?
                              Child, come out to us,
     since you know what your father has in mind.
     Bring your brother, Orestes, with you.
     Wrap him in the folds of your robe to keep him warm.
(Enter Iphigenia with Orestes.)
     She is here already. See how she listens,
     always obedient to her father. I see it's up to me
     to speak out, for her and for myself.   1310

AGAMEMNON
     Daughter, you're crying. Where is that shining face
     that met me such a short while ago?
     Now you look down and shroud your eyes with your shawl.

CLYTEMNESTRA
     O gods! Is there no beginning or end
     to my misfortune? It is one snarled thread
     from first to last.

AGAMEMNON
                         How you both look at me!
     Like some conspiracy of pain. The same
     contorted features—what might be astonishment,
     or blame.

CLYTEMNESTRA
                    Here is a question for you, husband.
     The truth, now. You owe it to me.   1320

AGAMEMNON
     You make it sound as if you had to wring
     the truth from me. Would I give you anything less?

CLYTEMNESTRA

    Tell me then—your daughter and mine—
    is it your intention to murder her?

AGAMEMNON

    Take care! What are you saying? Someone
    has poisoned your mind with vile accusations.
(shaking his head as if to clear it of the sight)
    And worse than your words are the images
    they call up.
(nearly aside)
           Doom hangs over me. That is my fate.

CLYTEMNESTRA

    And hers and mine. One end for all three.

AGAMEMNON

    But whom have I harmed?

CLYTEMNESTRA

                Can you ask that?   1330
    Do you have no sense of what you've done?

AGAMEMNON *(aside)*

    Then my secret lies open—as a grave.

CLYTEMNESTRA

    I know everything. I've taken pains to learn it!
    Your plot against us, the crime you plan.
    You don't deny it. No, you confess it
    with your silence. Your groans bear witness against you.
    Don't bother to speak.

AGAMEMNON

              I have nothing to say.
    Why add to my shame with lies?

CLYTEMNESTRA

                              Listen to me.
From now on there won't be hints to help you along
or riddles to make sense of. Only straight talk.   1340
Let me start, as I should, with what I can never
forgive, that you took me by force. That I went
to the marriage altar with you against my will.
You killed Tantalus, my husband, so you could take
his place. You tore the living infant from my breast—
horrible!—and smashed his head on the stones
beneath your feet. So my shining brothers,
my protectors, came galloping to my aid
on the whitest horses and made war on you.
But you fell at my father's feet and begged him,   1350
and Tyndareus took pity on you.
He raised you up and gave me to you and I—
I was reconciled to become your wife.
And a good wife I've been. You yourself
can swear to that. Unresisting in bed,
yet undemanding, too, no wanton.
The dowry I brought added to your wealth,
and my thrift kept it all intact. I have made
your house a place of peace for you. You go off
without a care and come home gladly. Good luck,   1360
isn't it, to find such a wife? When there's no lack
of worthless ones you could have had. And I gave you
this infant son you prize, and our three daughters,
all your children.

                         Now you will snatch one from me,
again, brutally. If I asked you why you want
to end this life you began, what could you tell me?
Should I say it for you? To return Helen
to Menelaus! Do you call this glory—
to make up a harlot's ransom in our children's blood?

If it were, we'd bargain away what we love most   1370
for everything despicable. Only think!

If you go off to war—who knows for how many years?—
and leave me in charge, would you expect me
to keep these halls safe for you, when each room
where I saw her stand, each chair she might have sat in,
kept bringing her back to me?
                                         I could only spend
my lonely days in tears, mourning her
forever. "Oh, child," in my mind I'd say to her,
"your father, who gave you life, took it back,
he who should have loved you best." And I'd level   1380
a debt of vengeance against this house.

Not that I or the children who are left
need a pretext to meet you at the door
with the only appropriate greeting! Heaven help me!
You have turned me into a traitor—to you
or to myself. And, after this, if you let her die,
how would you still pray to the gods?
What blessing could you, a child-killer, ask?

If you set out in shame, who will celebrate
your homecoming? It would be hypocrisy   1390
to wish you well. We'd be making fools of the gods
if we asked them to honor murderers.
And would you expect a child of yours
to come willingly into your arms? Could you
look any one of them in the eye after what
you'd done? Maybe you haven't thought of this.
Does it mean anything to you? Only power
moves you. To wave a scepter or a sword
before a mob and have them follow you.
You should have made a counter-offer when the seer   1400
came to you. "Achaeans! Do you mean
to sail against Troy? Then let's cast lots to see
whose daughter dies." That is justice. Not choosing
your own child for the sacrifice. The quarrel
is Menelaus'. Let him kill his daughter Hermione

for her mother's sake. I have been faithful to you,
yet you are making me plead for my daughter's life
while that harlot, my sister, will bring her own child
back to Sparta in luxury. Isn't this true?
Show me the law that rewards evil and condemns   1410
the virtuous to death. Do what is right.
Let our child live.

CHORUS

                    Listen to her, Agamemnon.
What blame lies in sparing your daughter's life?

IPHIGENIA

    O father, if I were Orpheus, I could pluck
a few strings of the lyre and sing the very stones
up from the ground to follow me. I'd be able
to move anyone or anything to my will.
But I have only these poor tears to persuade you.
Let me cling to your knees like a vine with this body
my mother bore you. Would you banish it so soon   1420
from the earth? Daylight is still sweet to me.
Don't make me turn my back on all I desire
to enter that gloom where nothing is. I was first
to call you father and you to call me child.
Your lap was my throne, and I sat embracing you,
and you me. You said to me, "My dear, one day
you will marry, with my blessing. I will see you
blooming and happy in your husband's house,
and all the care I have taken to raise you
will be rewarded." And I wound my fingers   1430
in your beard as I am doing now and answered you,
"Then you will be an old man. Gray hair will salt
this beard, and I will throw open the doors
of my husband's house to you. I will honor you
and say 'Welcome. This is your home now,
father. Let me repay you for your love and care

all the years of my childhood.'" I know that is how
we spoke to each other. If you remembered too,
you could not kill me. Not by Pelops and
your father, Atreus, not by my own mother,   1440
who stands here helplessly, who brought me
into the world in pain and in pain will watch me
be ripped from it unnaturally—no!

                                                     What part
did I play in Helen's rape? Why, father,
would I bring Paris here, so he could ruin me
as well? Look at me. Give me one glance, one kiss
at least, to take with me to remember you,
if this plea fails.

(turning to Orestes)

                                 Brother, you are not much help
to those who love you. Still, you can plead for your sister
with your tears. Join them to mine and beg our father   1450
for my life. Even an infant without understanding
knows wrong from right. Father, if he cannot
find words to speak, let his silence move you.
Together, we turn to you who gave us life,
a nursing baby and your grown daughter. Hear us
cry out to you—pity me! The light was made for us
to see by, but death reveals nothing. Only the mad
could prefer it. Why, a life spent in misery
is better than the most glorious death.

CHORUS

    O Helen, see the suffering you and your sins   1460
    have brought down on the line of Atreus!

AGAMEMNON

    I know where pity is called for and where
    it is wasted. Of course, I love my children, wife.
    I would not be human if I did not. What has
    been asked of me fills me with terror.

But it is as terrifying to refuse.
I must do this. Look around you. We are surrounded
by men in battle dress. Bronze-clad
kings of Greece stand between us and the sea.
How can they sail to Ilium to raze   1470
Troy's shining towers until this blood is shed?
The seer Calchas demands it. The Greek forces
are crying out for it. Can't you see,
they're mad to make their way to Troy
to avenge Helen's rape? No Greek wife is safe,
they say. Next, it will be their own sisters
and daughters, they say. And if they are kept
from satisfying this blood lust
among barbarians—if I refuse the goddess—
they will turn on Argos and slay our children   1480
in their beds, and us as well. Is this what you want?

(turning to Iphigenia)

Child, you think I'm Menelaus' flunkey.
But I haven't come to do his bidding.
The army is only so many city-states,
unless I hold it together for Greece's sake.
You see? It's not my choice. Her safety
depends on me, and on you, on what is done here.
You must die. Otherwise, she will weaken
and become the prey of any foreign tyrant.

CLYTEMNESTRA
My child too. Daughter!

(to Chorus)

                      And you who are   1490
daughters of someone, somewhere. You will live
while she dies. Mourn her! See how her father
loves her. He will hand her over to Hades,
then go off himself to war.

IPHIGENIA
                        Mother,
is all lost, then? It must be. Your cries echo my cries,
a mournful duet that fate cannot hear.
The sun will come up and my eyes will not open.
Already, a shadow has fallen over them,
cast by Mt. Ida in Phrygia, that snowy peak
where Priam set out his infant son to die.   1500
But he lived, this Paris of Ida. A cowherd
found him and took him in. And he himself
became a herdsman, living far from men, among cattle.
Oh, if only mountaintops never warmed to spring,
or no human heart had melted at the sight of him!

But the fountains unfroze and a silver spray
played over the meadows, tempting goddesses
to set down their feet. They came
for Paris' judgment: First, the goddess of love,
eyes shining, sure of beguiling him,   1510
then Athena, with her bow and spear,
even Hera, the sky's queen. Hermes stood by
to bring heaven the verdict. That is the contest
where I won death and the Danaans' glory.

O mother, Artemis has me in her sights.
I am the first poor prey of the hunt.
My own father has offered me to her.
Heaven knows, I am his to give,
his pitiful daughter. Then he will sail away.

Helen, your face was my first sight of evil,   1520
your name is a lingering bitterness on my tongue.
What have you brought us but suffering and shame?
I will die because of you. My father
will butcher me before the eyes of all Greece.

If only Aulis' harbor had never sheltered them
when the ships swept down on pine wings, making their way
to plunder Troy. If only Zeus had not breathed his breath
into the Euripus against a wind
to carry them away. For he chooses which sails
to fill with mighty gusts and which to chain   1530
where they stand. Our men's days are spent waiting.
This is your doing, Tyndareus' daughter.

CHORUS

    Oh, sad, to come all that way, and you
    a king's daughter, with only ruin awaiting you.

IPHIGENIA

    Mother, who are these men hurrying toward us?

CLYTEMNESTRA

    See, daughter, it is the one you have come to meet,
    Thetis' child.

IPHIGENIA *(pulling at the tent flap)*

              Women, open up, let me inside
    to hide myself!

CLYTEMNESTRA

           Why are you running away?
    Come out and greet him.

IPHIGENIA

             I am ashamed to,
    I don't want him to see me.

CLYTEMNESTRA

            Why shouldn't he?   1540
    He knows you are here.

IPHIGENIA

>But I came because I thought
he chose me. Now I know he doesn't want me.

CLYTEMNESTRA

>This is no time for modesty. Show yourself.
>You're no languishing rose, posing to attract him.
>Fate has robbed you of that delicacy.

(Exit Iphigenia.)

>Hide yourself, then. Do what you like.

(Enter Achilles.)

ACHILLES

>Unlucky woman! Clytemnestra, Leda's child—

CLYTEMNESTRA

>Unlucky, certainly. This day has seen to that.

ACHILLES

>Can you hear the shouts of the Argives?

CLYTEMNESTRA

>What is happening? What are they saying?   1550

ACHILLES

>It concerns your daughter.

CLYTEMNESTRA

>   And what concerns her,
>but danger, ruin? I hear it in your voice.

ACHILLES

>"She must die!" they are crying.

CLYTEMNESTRA

                              Doesn't anyone
    want to save her?

ACHILLES

                    I spoke up in the midst
    of the commotion. But it was risky.

CLYTEMNESTRA
    Did they threaten you?

ACHILLES

                              They said they would stone me.

CLYTEMNESTRA
    For defending my daughter?

ACHILLES

                         For that, exactly.

CLYTEMNESTRA
    But who would dare lay a hand on you?

ACHILLES
     The whole Greek army, it seems.

CLYTEMNESTRA

                              But the Myrmidons,
    your own forces—

ACHILLES

                    They were first to turn against me.   1560

CLYTEMNESTRA *(aside)*
    If that is so, my daughter, we are lost.

ACHILLES

I called her my bride and they jeered at me.

CLYTEMNESTRA

They didn't believe you?

ACHILLES

"You can't kill her," I said.
"She has been promised to me."

CLYTEMNESTRA

That is the truth.

ACHILLES

"Agamemnon sent for her," I said.

CLYTEMNESTRA

And he did, all the way from Argos.

ACHILLES

But they shouted me down.

CLYTEMNESTRA

Worthless scum!

ACHILLES

This isn't the last of it. I'll stand by you.

CLYTEMNESTRA

What—one man take on a whole army?

ACHILLES

Here, you see my armor bearers.
(points to two servants)

CLYTEMNESTRA

                    Heaven help you.   1570

ACHILLES

    Oh, heaven will. I'll have the gods' blessings.

CLYTEMNESTRA

    Then we can count on you? You will see
    that she isn't brought to the altar?

ACHILLES

    Not while I have a breath in me.

CLYTEMNESTRA

                  And when you haven't
    will anyone come to take her?

ACHILLES

               Thousands will come,
    and Odysseus will lead them.

CLYTEMNESTRA

    The son of Sisyphus?

ACHILLES

          That one, yes.

CLYTEMNESTRA

    Did he volunteer or was he ordered to take her?

ACHILLES

    The army chose him, but he was willing.

CLYTEMNESTRA

    A wicked choice, theirs and his, to murder her.   1580

IPHIGENIA

 Land that nurtured me, where I grew to be
 the beacon light of Greece. For you I die gladly.

CHORUS

 Your glory will brighten that place for all time.

IPHIGENIA

 And day, that I love, that is lit by the gods,
 the world's torch. I must live without you, a strange,
    dark world.   1740
 Sunlight that has grown dear to me, farewell.

CHORUS LEADER

 Now, let her pass, the sacker of cities,
 the leveler of Troy. Her yellow hair
 is starred with flowers.
 Her skin has been sprinkled
 with purifying waters. She is on her way.

 Soon her life will rush out across the altar
 when the knife bites her throat.
(to Iphigenia)
 And while in sacrifice
 your father is pouring out the lustral waters,   1750
 warriors in their thousands
 will be straining toward Troy.

SECOND VOICE

 Praise the hunter-goddess.
 Sing out her name!
(to Iphigenia)
 Girl, what greatness Greece gains with your loss!
 O Zeus' daughter,
 divine slaughterer of human and animal,
 guide the fleet safely

to that far, treacherous shore.
Bless our king. He acted wisely.   1760
And bless our armies.
Prepare them for the good fight.
(Dark stage—one dim light. Pause. Enter Messenger.)

MESSENGER

Clytemnestra, Tyndareus' daughter,
Come out from your tent. I have a tale to tell you.

CLYTEMNESTRA

I come because you call me, but I am afraid
of your news. Do you have a fresh horror
to lay at my feet?

MESSENGER

Not that. A wonder.
It thrilled me to see it, and I will relate it to you
with what can only be great joy—

CLYTEMNESTRA

Say it, then.
And quickly.

MESSENGER

I will tell you as fast   1770
as my tongue allows, mistress,
except where I must stop and try to put
my thoughts in order. For it was something
so new to my eyes—. Well, we came to the grove
of Artemis, the flowering meadow
where the Greek troops stood. We led in your daughter
and they gathered around her. Your husband
couldn't bear to look. He only groaned
and lifted his arm up to shield his eyes.

But she went to him and stood beside him, saying,   1780
lowers himself to the ground, half-kneeling, half-raising himself
                    animatedly toward Clytemnestra)
"Father, you asked me to come? I am here.
I will give myself to you for our country's sake,
for Greece. Lead me to the goddess' altar.
And, because heaven requires it, sacrifice
my body so the army can prosper.
Then, if the gods allow it, let my death
bring you victory and peace.
(as if motioning back attendants)
                    No! Stand back.
No one put a hand on me," she cried out
when the attendants came. "Alone, unflinching,
I will lower myself to the slaying stone   1790
and yield my neck to the knife."
                    Your daughter
spoke these words with such a true heart
that each man who heard was overcome.
They called her hero, marveling at her courage.
Then the priest Talthybius, whose job it was,
raised his hands and a reverent silence
fell over them. And Calchas, the seer,
reached into a golden basket for the knife
and drew it out. He put a laurel crown
on the girl's head. Peleus' son, Achilles,   1800
took the basket and the bowl of lustral water
and circled the altar, crying, "Artemis,
divine huntress, killer of wild things.
You twirl heaven's light through the unknown dark,
making a path for us. Accept this offering
from the Achaeans and their king, Agamemnon,
the blood that flows from a pure maiden's neck.

"Grant us the wind we pray for. Let our galleys
go unhindered. Point our spears at last toward Troy."

Then the sons of Atreus and all the host   1810
stood bowing their heads. The priest spoke the prayer
and took up the knife. He scanned the child's neck
for the exact point to strike. Anguish gripped me
and my head sunk to my chest—when suddenly—
a miracle! Though each man plainly heard
the sound of the blow, we looked up to see
that the girl—had vanished! The priest cried out
and we, all of us, echoed his cry. Here,
unsought, past all belief, was a sign from the gods.

For on the ground lay a huge, horned deer,   1820
quite beautiful, really, gasping for breath
as its blood streamed across the altar.
Then Calchas shouted with joy, as you'd imagine,
"Kings and princes of Greece. Do you see
this mountain deer laid down before us?
The goddess has chosen her own victim.
An animal is more pleasing to her
than the maiden. She prefers not to spill
royal blood. It's clear then, she's satisfied
with our sacrifice. Let every man give thanks!   1830
Now quickly board your ships. This very day
we will fly from Aulis harbor and cross
the surging Aegean." So when the fire god's flames
had reduced the great deer carcass to ash,
Calchas prayed for the army's safe return.

Agamemnon sent me off then to tell you
all that happened and to impress on you
his heaven-sent good fortune and the fame
it has won him throughout Greece. I speak
as a witness. I swear to what I saw.   1840
Without a doubt, your daughter was raised up
to Olympus. Forget your grief and anger
at your lord. How can we explain to ourselves

the gods' actions? Only say that they save
those they love. Today, before my eyes, your child
who seemed dead has been brought back to life.

CHORUS

This messenger has touched you with glory.
He says your child will live again, and with the gods.

CLYTEMNESTRA

Daughter, is it true a god has carried you off?
Then how can I say goodbye? Should I believe   1850
what they tell me, or is it some sweet lie
meant to draw the bitterness from my heart?

CHORUS

Here is Agamemnon. He has come himself
to make you believe the miracle.

AGAMEMNON

Wife, be happy at our daughter's fate. She is in
the company of the gods. Go now,
take your youngest home. The ships are moving out to sea.
It may be long years before we meet again,
not until I return victorious from Troy.

CHORUS

Farewell, son of Atreus. Now there is nothing   1860
to stop you. Pass safely through the battle strife
and fill your arms with the glittering spoils of Troy.
(*Exit all.*)

Rhesus

Translated by
George Economou

Translator's Preface

Th'Atrides watching, wake the other Peeres,
And (in the Fort, consulting of their feares)
Two kings they send, most stout and honord most,
For royall skowts into the Trojan host:
Who, meeting Dolon (Hector's bribed spie)
Take him, and learne how all the Quarters lie.
He told them, in the Thracian regiment
Of rich king Rhesus, and his royal Tent—
Striving for safetie, but they end his strife
And rid poore Dolon of a dangerous life.
Then with digressive wyles, they use their force
On Rhesus' life and take his snowie horse.
　　　—George Chapman, The Tenthe Booke of *Homer's Iliad*,
　　　　　The Argument

A play about losers, Euripides' *Rhesus* has been treated itself as a loser of a play in our time. Some modern scholars, in fact, have advocated the loss of its attribution to Euripides, though his authorship is well-attested in antiquity. The grounds for this argument have been that the play is so anomalous and defective as tragedy as to render its creation by a great artist unthinkable. Even many of those who acknowledge its authenticity seek excuses for its "failings" by pointing out that it is a very early composition, if not the first play Euripides ever wrote. It has been compared often to another early work of the playwright's *Cyclops*, which is the only complete satyr play extant. This perception of *Rhesus* as an example of Euripides' artistic immaturity, marked by its affinities with the conventions of the funny, cruel satyr play, has had an isolating if not alienating effect on its standing among the rest of Euripides' tragedies. Yet, as Anne Pippin Burnett has argued, the play's odd singularity, defined by its hatred of war and debunking of heroism, its scorn for the small, mean, and ugly ways of men, and even its apparent distrust and ridicule of the conventions of traditional tragedy, makes a better case for than against the play's originality and authenticity. Though it will probably never escape its status as an egregious example of Euripidean tragedy, *Rhesus* deserves to be accepted on its own terms. It may be, as it were, the black goat of the flock, and it may, for better or worse, stand apart from the rest, but its strange bleating can also be music to our ears.

Like *Cyclops*, *Rhesus* is based on a well-known episode in Homer. Adaptations respectively of the ninth book of the *Odyssey* (the Polyphemus episode) and the tenth book of the *Iliad* (the Doloneia), the satyr play and the early tragedy stand together in their unusual, direct dependence on Homeric sources for their plots. One of their strongest elements in common is an Odysseus who effectively displays the cunning resolve that enriched and complicated his stature among the heroes of antiquity. In one play he outwits a dim one-eyed giant of a loud-mouthed brute amid the antics of old Silenus and his satyrs. In the other he leads Diomedes in a night raid through a military camp in disarray, undoing a pathetic, self-serving would-be savior of his country and a noble sounding young warrior, also perceived as a savior, whose specific destiny is to be set up for a fall.

The individual fates of Dolon and Rhesus, however, foretell the fate of the entire Trojan cause. Shifting the point of view to that of the Trojans in the course of a single night, Euripides represents misjudgment and overreaching in a parade of individuals who are literally feeling their way in the dark. Dolon is outdone by the Odysseus he says he will kill in the craft (*dolos*) for which he is named. Rhesus brags about killing Achilles and Odysseus and conquering all of Greece before he lays eyes on any one of them. Hector keeps changing his mind and losing his temper while clinging to his dream of heroically driving his enemies away. And the Chorus bungles its way through its assigned night watch, allowing the perpetrators of the Thracian slaughter to slip through their fingers. Even Odysseus and Diomedes must have their ambitions checked by Athena, who diverts their murderous energy away from Hector and Paris and directs it toward Rhesus and his sleeping troops.

It is not surprising that a major paradigm of the play's settling of accounts should consist of equal doses of obliquity and irony. Dolon, whose puffed up, doomed mission has no significant impact on the ensuing action, would have Achilles' horses (Hector has also thought about possessing them) as the reward for his self-proclaimed future success as a spy in a wolfskin. And Rhesus, despite his god-given potential for glory—if only he can live through this ill-fated night—ends up a butchered corpse who has also accomplished nothing, his swan-white horses stolen by Odysseus. Is it not characteristic of Euripides that the prize of chariot horses, traditional symbols of the heroic life, are reduced to the role of common denominator in a trade-off between vainglorious intentions and steely-nerved deception?

As in my translation of the *Cyclops* two decades ago, I have tried to represent the speech of Euripides' characters as I would imagine hearing it spoken by contemporary actors. I have divided some of the speeches of the Chorus, particularly those designated in the Greek text as belonging to a "Semi-Chorus," into individual speeches of a First and Second Chorist in order to connect the discourse of the Chorus more precisely to both its own actions and the actions of the other characters in the play. Readers and directors should feel free to alter this innovation to suit their conceptions of the work, just as they should take most of the stage directions as suggested answers to questions the play raises about its own performance. For example, I have suggested that Dolon enter with Aeneas, but he could just as easily be on stage already. Like his counterparts in life, he is a nobody who comes out of nowhere but always seems to be available when opportunities arise.

The Greek text does not tell us exactly which Muse Rhesus' mother is, though some commentators have identified her as Terpsichore and others as Euterpe. I suspect Euripides thought her identity was obvious, though we may be at a loss for an exact answer to this question, too. Perhaps a more meaningful question for us to ponder concerning the quality and playability of *Rhesus* is one raised by another question, the well-known one asked by Goethe about its author in his diary a few months before his death: "Has any nation ever produced a dramatist who would deserve to hand him his slippers?" Does such praise extend to the work that follows? As ever, it is the reader's call.

The text followed for this translation is that edited by James Diggle, *Euripides*, Vol. 3 (Oxford: Clarendon Press, 1994). Textual notes in Diggle's *Euripidea: Collected Essays* (Oxford: Clarendon Press, 1994) were also consulted. For edifying further reading, see Anne Pippin Burnett, "*Rhesus*: Are Smiles Allowed?" in *Directions in Euripidean Criticism: A Collection of Essays*, ed. Peter Burian (Durham, N.C.: Duke University Press, 1985), pp. 13–51.

Cast

CHORUS OF TROJAN GUARDS
HECTOR, son of Priam king of Troy
AENEAS, Trojan leader
DOLON
SHEPHERD
RHESUS, Thracian leader
ODYSSEUS, Greek hero, king of Ithaca
DIOMEDES, Greek hero
ATHENA, the goddess
PARIS (Alexander), son of Priam and Hecuba who abducted
    Helen to Troy
CHARIOTEER
MUSE, mother of Rhesus
NONSPEAKING
    Thracian warriors
    Trojans

*(It is night in the Trojan camp. The Chorus of Trojan guards, on
    fourth nightwatch duty, enters in search of Hector.)*

FIRST CHORIST
    Let's find where Hector sleeps.

SECOND CHORIST
    Is anyone awake, the king's bodyguard
    or an armor bearer?

FIRST CHORIST
    Here is a new report for him.
    We are the night's fourth watch,
    and protect the entire army.

SECOND CHORIST
> Raise your head and rest it on your arm.
> Open your lids and unseal your fierce stare.

FIRST CHORIST
> Rise from your bed of leaves,
> Hector, and now hear this.   10

HECTOR
> Who goes there—friend or foe?
> What's the password? Speak up!
> Who approaches out of the night
> to where I sleep? Answer me.

CHORUS
> Sentries of the army.

HECTOR
>   And what's upset you?

CHORUS
> Don't be afraid.

HECTOR
>   I am not afraid.
> It isn't an ambush by night?

CHORUS
>   Not at all.

HECTOR
>   Then why,
> if we're not to mobilize by night,
> do you abandon your post and stir up the company?
> Can't you see the Argive spears   20
> are so near us, here where we sleep in our armor?

CHORUS

Strophe

Arm yourself Hector, hurry
to where your allies sleep.
Rouse them to take up their weapons.
Dispatch friends to fly throughout the company.
Hitch the horses to the curb chains.
Who will go to Polydamas, Panthous' son,
or to Europa's, Sarpedon, chief of the Lycians?
Where are the sacrifice makers?
Where are the leaders of the light-armed troops?   30
Where are the Phrygian archers?
They should be stringing their horn-tipped bows.

HECTOR

Your message sounds partly alarming,
partly encouraging. None of it is clear.
Can it be that Cronian Pan's lash
has you quivering in fear? Why do you desert your watch
to stir up the army? What is this noise?
What is your message? You talk a lot
but say nothing plainly.

CHORUS

Antistrophe

The Argive army has started fires, Hector,   40
they've lit up the whole night,
and their ships' lines flash in the firelight.
Their entire army goes noisily
in the darkness to Agamemnon's tent,
eager for some new command;
for never before has this seaborne
army been so completely routed.
Uncertain about what might happen,

I bring you my report, so that
you may never say I'm to blame.   50

HECTOR

Your coming is timely, though your message is one of fear.
These Greeks plan to row away from here secretly by night
out of my sight, and thus make their getaway.
That's how their night fires strike me.
O God, I am a lion robbed of his prey
at the moment of success as I was about to destroy
the Argive army with one sweep of my spear.
For if the sun's bright lamps hadn't shut down,
I would not have held back my triumphant blows
until I had torched their ships and come to their tents,   60
killing Achaeans with this deadly hand.
I was on fire, eager to sustain my offensive
through the night with my god-given momentum.
But these wise men, these seers who know heaven's mind,
prevailed on me to wait for daybreak.
By then no Achaean would be left on dry land.
But the enemy won't wait for plans made by priests.
In the dark the fugitive grows strong.
Pass the message to all the army quickly—
to shake off sleep and take up arms.   70
The enemy, even as he jumps aboard ship,
will be hit in the back and stain the ladders red.
Let the rest be captured, snared and tied up
to learn well how to work our Phrygian fields.

CHORUS

Not so fast, Hector, you'd act before you know.
We're not at all sure these men are running away.

HECTOR

Then why does the Argive army light fires?

CHORUS
I don't know, but in my heart I have misgivings.

HECTOR
If this scares you, then anything would.

CHORUS
The enemy never before lit fires like these.   80

HECTOR
And never before was so disgracefully routed.

CHORUS
Your achievement. So you decide now what's next.

HECTOR
One simple order against the enemy—to arms.

CHORUS
Aeneas approaches running fast
like one who has news to give his friends.
(Enter Aeneas, Dolon, and other Trojans.)

AENEAS
Hector, why does the nightwatch
come into camp to your quarters, scared
and disturbing the army with talk in the night?

HECTOR
Aeneas, suit up in your armor.

AENEAS
Hold on! Why? Is there news our opponents   90
have set a trap for us by night?

HECTOR

No, they retreat, boarding their ships.

AENEAS

Can you give me proof?

HECTOR

All night long they've set burning torches.
I don't think they'll wait for morning,
but lighting up their well-benched ships
they'll depart this country and flee for home.

AENEAS

And so you arm yourself to do something about this?

HECTOR

Yes, as they flee, leaping on to their ships,
my spear will stop them. I'll come down hard on them.   100
It would be a disgrace and, worse, an evil dishonor
when God has given us enemies who've lost their fight
to let them escape when they've done us so much harm.

AENEAS

Too bad you don't plan as well as you fight.
But so it goes, one man can't have it all,
do everything. Different men, different gifts,
and yours is fighting, while others are good at strategy.
Excited, you hear about the lit fires
and the Achaeans' flight, and you plan to lead the army
over the trenches in the middle of the night.   110
Yet if once you've crossed the deep, yawning ditch,
you meet an enemy with no intention of leaving this land,
but squares off against you with raised spears,
I'm afraid you'll not return home if they defeat you.
How can a retreating army pass over palisades?

How can charioteers drive over the causeways
without smashing up? Without shattering their cars' axles?
Even if you win, there is still Achilles, held in reserve,
and he won't let you torch their ships
or take Achaeans prisoner, as you hope.   120
The man's on fire and has towering valor.
No, better to let our army sleep in peace
on their shields away from the strife of battle.
Send a volunteer to spy on the enemy—
that's my advice. And if they're really fleeing,
we fall upon their army with all we've got.
But if these bonfires are part of a trick,
we'll find out the enemy's designs from our spy.
And then plan our response. My lord, this is what I think.

CHORUS

Strophe

This is what I think, too. Change your mind and agree.   130
I don't care for a general's command if it wavers.
What could be better than if one who can run
went to have a look at their ships?
Moved in close to find out why the enemy
has set fires where their ships lie prow to prow.

HECTOR

You win, since you all want this.
Go and quiet our allies. Perhaps the army
has been unsettled by hearing our assembly in the night.
I will dispatch a man to spy on the enemy.
And if we find out this is a trick,   140
you'll hear about it and come to our conference.
But if they're rushing to sail away,
listen for the trumpet's blast. Be ready.
Because I will not wait, but this very night
I will attack the Argive force at the cables of their ships.

AENEAS

Send your man right away. Your plan makes sense now.
And if need be, look for me to be as brave as you.
(*Aeneas exits.*)

HECTOR

Is there any Trojan in this council
who wants to spy on the Argive ships?
What son of our country wants to be its benefactor?   150
Anybody talking? Now I can't be expected
to do everything for my city and her friends.

DOLON

For my homeland, I will gladly take
the risk of scouting the Argive ships.
I will reveal all the Achaeans' plans to you
when I return. I accept the assignment with these conditions.

HECTOR

No wonder you are called wily Dolon, and patriot, too.
You have now doubled the glory
of your father's house.

DOLON

If it is right to work hard, shouldn't hard work   160
result in recompense? For work that anticipates
reward is done with double pleasure.

HECTOR

Absolutely. I wouldn't have it any other way.
Name your price—but forget my royal prerogatives.

DOLON

I've no great desire for any of your royal prerogatives.

HECTOR

Then marry one of Priam's daughters and be my brother-in-law.

DOLON

I wouldn't want to marry above my station.

HECTOR

I can offer gold, if that's the prize you want.

DOLON

We have that at home. We lack nothing the good life asks.

HECTOR

Then which of Ilium's hidden treasures would you like?   170

DOLON

Round up the Achaeans and then reward me.

HECTOR

I will. But don't ask me for the captains of their fleet.

DOLON

You can kill them. I won't ask you for Menelaus' life.

HECTOR

Are you asking me to give you Ajax?

DOLON

Such well-born hands are bad for field work.

HECTOR

Then which Achaean would you like to hold for ransom?

DOLON

As I just said, we have enough gold in our house.

HECTOR

Well then, come and choose for yourself from the spoils.

DOLON

> Hang such things for the gods on their temples.

HECTOR

> What more than these things can you ask of me?   180

DOLON

> Achilles' horses. A high price should be paid
> to the man who risks his life on the gods' roll of the dice.

HECTOR

> So, we are rivals for those horses.
> They are immortal, were sired by immortals
> to bear the impetuous son of Peleus.
> Poseidon, king of the sea, broke and reared them.
> He gave them to Peleus, they say.
> Yet I will not betray hopes I raised. I give them to you,
> Achilles' team, an outstanding possession for your house.

DOLON

> I thank you. In receiving them my brave heart   190
> wins the finest reward in all of Phrygia.
> But don't be jealous. There's so much more
> for you, the best in the land, to enjoy.

(Hector moves away from center stage to the back, perhaps to resume his rest.)

CHORUS

Antistrophe

> The contest is great, your goal is great.
> For sure, you'll be blessed if you can win.
> The work that comes is glorious.
> Still, marrying into the royal family would have been daring.
> May Justice see to what the gods give you,
> just as it seems you'll get what you deserve from men.

DOLON

    I'll be ready to go, once I've stopped by my house   200
    to suit up in the appropriate gear.
    From there I'll make my run to the Argive ships.

CHORUS

    Tell us what you plan to change into.

DOLON

    Something proper to my task and my stealthy moves.

CHORUS

    Craftiness is to be learned from a crafty man.
    So tell, how will you equip yourself?

DOLON

    I'll pull a wolfskin over my back.
    Fit the animal's gaping jaws on my head.
    I'll fasten its forepaws to my hands
    and its hind legs to my own legs. Then I will play   210
    the four-footed wolf, fooling the enemies who track me,
    beside the ditch and the ships lined up on the beach.
    As soon as my feet touch an isolated spot, I'll stand
    and walk on two. And that's the "Dolon dodge."

CHORUS

    May Maia's son Hermes, prince of tricksters,
    be with you in your coming and going.
    You know your stuff, and only need a little luck.

DOLON

    Oh, I'll get back all right. And with dead Odysseus'
    head to show, or maybe Diomedes'—
    proof for you that Dolon   220
    got through to the Argive ships.

Yes, before day breaks over this land,
I'll come home with blood on my hands.
(Dolon exits.)

CHORUS

Strophe

Lord of Thymbraeum, of Delos, and of Lycia,
whose shrine you protect,
Apollo, O shining brow, come with your bow tonight.
Be this man's savior, guide,
captain, and rally Dardanus' children,
O almighty power who so long ago
built the walls of Troy.   230

Antistrophe

Let him scout the Greek army
come to their seafarers
and return to the altars of his father's house in Troy.
Let him one day drive the Phthian horse-drawn car,
those horses the sea god
gave to Peleus, Aeacus' son,
after our chief has wasted the Achaean war force.

Strophe

Let him, because he alone for country dared
go down to the harbor to spy.
I admire his spirit, for very few   240
are so brave when the city
is tossed on a stormy, open sea.
We still have stout hearts in Phrygia,
some courage in our warfare. Only a bragging
Mysian would scoff at our assistance.

Antistrophe

Which Achaean will our prowling killer
strike in their camp as he moves about
on all fours like an animal?
Let him kill Menelaus.
Or slaughter Agamemnon and drop his head   250
into wailing Helen's hands, his evil sister-in-law.
For against our city and our Trojan land
he brought an army in a thousand ships.

(A shepherd runs in and Hector comes forward to take his message.)

SHEPHERD

My lord, may I always be such a messenger,
and bring you news you'll be glad to hear.

HECTOR

What boors and dim-wits these country bumpkins are.
Do you think it's appropriate to bring intelligence
about your flocks to war lords like us? Well, it isn't.
Don't you know where my house is, or my father's throne?
Proclaim your sheep's prosperity there.   260

SHEPHERD

Granted, we sheepherders can be louts.
Nonetheless, I bring you welcome news.

HECTOR

Stop talking to me about what's new on the farm.
We are armed and have battles to fight.

SHEPHERD

And I have news about exactly such things.
A princely man who commands thousands
comes as your friend and ally to our country.

HECTOR

    What ancestral land has he emptied of its manpower?

SHEPHERD

    Thrace. His father's name is Strymon.

HECTOR

    Rhesus. You say he's set foot in Troy?   270

SHEPHERD

    Correct. You've saved me half of what I have to say.

HECTOR

    But why does he travel across Mount Ida's meadows?
    Why the detour from the wagon road on the wide open plain?

SHEPHERD

    Of that I'm not sure, but I can make a guess.
    It's no mean thing to happen upon an army by night,
    when you've heard the plain is full of belligerent enemies.
    We country boys, who live on Ida's rocky slopes,
    the hearth and heartland of our nation, were frightened
    by his coming in the night through oak wood and wild life.
    The Thracian army made a lot of noise as it poured through.   280
    In panic-struck amazement we drove the flocks
    up to the ridges, suspecting Greeks out for plunder
    had come to raid your livestock.
    But when their speech, which did not sound like Greek,
    was clear to us, we were no longer afraid.
    I stood in the road in front of their king's scouts.
    Speaking Thracian, I asked them
    about their leader and whose son he is
    who comes as an ally toward Priam's city.
    After I had heard everything I wanted to know,   290
    I just stood there. And then I see him, Rhesus,

standing tall in his Thracian chariot like a god.
A golden yoke-beam joined the necks
of his colts, which glistened whiter than snow.
Slung on his shoulders, his gold-plated buckler glowed.
A bronze gorgon, like the one on the aegis of the goddess,
was bound to the horses' frontlet shields,
whose countless bells jangled a fearful message.
The size of his army you could not come close
to reckoning. Way too big to take in with one look.   300
There were many horsemen and targeteers in line,
archers with unfeathered arrows, and a throng
of light-armed troops that followed, all in Thracian dress.
Such is the man who stands as Troy's ally.
Neither by flight nor by fighting him
can Peleus' son Achilles find a way out.

CHORUS

When the gods' support is steadfast,
fortune's downhill slide can be reversed.

HECTOR

So now that I'm ahead, and Zeus
stands on our side, I gain all kinds of friends.   310
Who needs them? Those who in the past
wouldn't help out, when relentless Ares
ripped the sails of this land with his great blasts?
Rhesus has shown what kind of friend he is to Troy.
He comes to the feast, but wasn't there
with his spear to help the hunters take the quarry.

CHORUS

You're right to reproach and disdain such friends.
But accept those who are willing to help our city.

HECTOR

We who have saved Ilium all along are enough.

CHORUS

Are you sure you have defeated this enemy?   320

HECTOR

Yes, I'm sure, and god's sunrise will bear it out.

CHORUS

Beware of the future, for god often turns things around.

HECTOR

I hate when friends come too late to be of help.
Yet since this man has already arrived, welcome him
as a stranger, not an ally, as guest to our table.
Priam's sons owe him no special favor.

CHORUS

My lord, an ally rejected can turn hostile.

SHEPHERD

The sight of him alone would scare the enemy.

HECTOR

Good advice—and your report is timely.
So as you say, then, messenger,   330
let this gold-armored Rhesus come as our ally.

CHORUS

Strophe

Adrasteia, Zeus' child Nemesis,
keep envy from my lips.
For all that I hold dear in my heart,
for all that I will speak.
You have come, O River-god's child.
At last you have come, and are welcome
here in our Phrygian courtyard.

You were sent by your mother Muse
and the fair-bridged River   340

Antistrophe

Strymon, who with the melodious
Muse, through his crystal clear
eddies' swirl in her lap,
begot your splendid manhood.
You come to me. You appear
like Zeus, driving dappled horses.
My country, O my Phrygia,
with god's help, now you will have a liberator,
a Zeus to protect you.

Strophe

Will our ancient Troy ever again see   350
the close of a long day's revel?
Or of love's companionship and promise
strummed on the harp as the wine cups
pass left to right in happy contest
while Atreus' sons make for Sparta
on the high sea far from Ilium's shores?
O friend, if only you could make this happen
with your hand and your spear
before you leave our home.

Antistrophe

Come, thrust your golden buckler   360
in the eyes of Peleus' son, Achilles.
Raise it up and athwart
the chariot's double rail. Urge your horses.
And with a quick move cast your double javelin.
None who stands against you
shall ever dance again on Argive Hera's plains.
But this earth will be only too glad

to take in his dead weight,
brought down by a Thracian death.
(Rhesus enters with a company of Thracian warriors.)
    He has come, O Thrace, great and noble king,   370
    this young lion you reared, the very image of a prince.
    Mark his gold-bound body's prowess.
    Hear the din of the ringing bells
    jangling from the handles of his shield.
    A god come to inspire you
    is this young stud, O Troy, an Ares
    out of Strymon and the singing Muse.

RHESUS

    I salute you, Hector, brave son of a brave father,
    lord of this land, and at this late date I greet you.
    I take joy in your success and in your position   380
    near your enemy's fortress. I come to help you
    demolish their ramparts and to burn their hollow ships.

HECTOR

    Son of the singing mother Muse
    and of Thrace's river Strymon, I always love
    to speak the truth and am no diplomat.
    You should have come to this country's aid
    a long, long time ago. For all your help,
    Troy would have fallen to these hostile Greeks.
    You can't say it was because your friends did not call
    that you didn't come, didn't help, didn't pay attention.   390
    What Phrygian herald or embassy
    did not come to ask you to help our city?
    What good gifts did we not send you?
    We are one race, barbarians both,
    and you still betrayed us to the Greeks.
    Yet with this hand I made you the great
    King of Thracians from a petty lord.
    Throughout Pangaeum and Paeonia
    I fought face to face with Thrace's bravest

and broke their line of shields. Their conquered people   400
I gave to you. And this great favor
you now spurn by coming late to help friends in distress.
Others, with no kinship to us at all,
have long stood by. Some of them have fallen
and lie in burial mounds, no small loyalty to our city.
And some, fully armed by their chariot teams,
withstand with manful endurance the cold blasts
or parching thirst god gives. They are not cozily bedded down
like you with long drinks toasting friendship's good times.
So, now you know Hector's freely spoken mind,   410
and that I fault you and say it to your face.

RHESUS

I am the same kind of man. I cut a straight
path through words. I, too, am no double-talking diplomat.
And I am more grieved than you by my absence
from your land, more pained at heart, more discontent.
But there's a land that borders mine, the Scythians',
and as I was on the point of coming to Ilium,
they attacked me from the other side. I had just reached
the shores of the Euxine Sea to transport my Thracian forces.
The soil there was soggy with spear-drawn   420
Scythian blood and Thracian, too, in common slaughter.
That was the mishap that blocked my approach
to Troy's plain to come to help you.
After I defeated them, I took their children hostage,
and set them annual tribute to bring to my house.
Then I sailed across the strait and am here,
passing the rest of the way over your frontier by foot—
not, as you taunt, taking long, deep drinks,
or sleeping in golden chambers.
I have known those icy blasts of wind   430
that sweep the Thracian sea and Paeonia,
have endured them sleepless in this cloak.
I may come late, but I come in time all the same.

You have been fighting for ten years now
and have gotten nowhere. Day after day
you shoot the dice of your war with the Argives.
But I will need only one day's sun
to destroy their walls, to burst upon their moorings,
and kill the Achaeans. The day after, I'm on my way home,
having made short work of your troubles.   440
Not one of you needs to lift a shield.
I will handle these Achaeans with their mighty boasts
and their spears, and put an end to them, even though I'm late.

CHORUS

Strophe

Yes, yes,
your cry is welcome, and so are you, sent by Zeus.
I only hope Zeus on highest
protects your words from invincible Envy.
For Argive warship never
before or to this day
brought a man as powerful as you.   450
How could Achilles stand up to your spear?
Or Ajax survive it? Tell me.
If I could only see the day, my lord,
when your lance will be raised
to avenge murderous deeds.

RHESUS

These things, to make up for my long absence,
I will do for you—Adrasteia keep fast what I say.
As soon as we have liberated this city
and you have chosen first fruits to devote to the gods,
I will march with you on Argive territory.   460
We will overcome all of Greece and demolish it.
Then it will be their turn to feel
what it's like to be in evil straits.

HECTOR

> If I could be rid of my present evil
> and rule a city secure again as it was in the past,
> I would be profoundly grateful to the gods.
> As for Argos and the fields of Greece,
> they are not as easy to vanquish as you think.

RHESUS

> Do they not say the best of the Achaeans are here?

HECTOR

> I wouldn't underestimate them. They're enough for me.   470

RHESUS

> So, then when we've killed them, aren't we finished?

HECTOR

> To mess up the present, look too far into the future.

RHESUS

> You seem content to take punishment and give none back.

HECTOR

> I rule a kingdom big enough for me.
> Now decide. Do you want the left or right wing
> or the center of the allied forces?
> Plant your shields and draw your lines.

RHESUS

> What I want, Hector, is to fight the enemy alone.
> But if you would be ashamed not to join in the burning
> of their ships, something you have worked so long for,   480
> line me up head to head with Achilles and his army.

HECTOR

> You won't be able to throw your hungry spear at him.

RHESUS

    The report says he also sailed to Troy.

HECTOR

    He did and is here. But he's angry
    with the general command and will not fight.

RHESUS

    Next to him who is most famous in their army?

HECTOR

    I think Ajax is in no way his inferior.
    And Tydeus' son, Diomedes. Then there's that glib and wily
    loud mouth, Odysseus—though his spirit is brave enough
    and he has abused our land more than any other man.   490
    It was he who came by night to Athena's shrine,
    stole her image and took it to the Argive ships.
    Recently, disguised as a lowly beggar,
    he passed through our walls, the whole time cursing
    the Argives, the very ones who sent him to spy on us.
    He murdered the guards and sentries of the gates
    and got away. He's always being spotted crouching
    by the altar of Apollo Thymbraeus, lurking near the city.
    He is a wicked piece of work we must put up with.

RHESUS

    A truly courageous man would never stoop to kill   500
    his foe by stealth. He rushes to meet him face to face.
    This man you say sits silently in wait
    and schemes away—him I will take alive
    and stand him up where the gates exit,
    impaled through the back, a feast for vultures.
    Such a death is a proper fate
    for one who robs the gods' temples.

HECTOR

    Make your camp now. It is night.
    Let me show you a place where your army

can spend the night, apart from us.   510
"Phoebus" is the password, if you need anything.
Memorize it and tell your Thracian men.
(to the Chorus)
You men, go forth beyond our lines
and keep a sharp lookout. Watch for Dolon,
our spy on the ships. If he's safe and sound,
he should be nearing the Trojan camp by now.
(Hector and Rhesus exit.)

CHORUS

     Strophe

Whose is the next watch?
Who follows us?
The night's first stars are setting
and the sevenway path of the Pleiades is rising.   520
In the heavens' center the Eagle hovers.
Wake up, why the delay?
Awake and take your watch.
Don't you see how the moon glows?
Dawn is near, dawn breaks,
and here is its harbinger star.

FIRST CHORIST
Who was called for the first watch?

SECOND CHORIST
Coroebus, they say, son of Mygdon.

FIRST CHORIST
And who after him?

SECOND CHORIST
The Paeonian troop awoke the Cilicians,   530
and the Mysians us.

FIRST CHORIST

  Isn't it time, then, that we go
  call the Lycians to the fifth watch
  according to the order of allotment?

CHORUS

  Antistrophe

  Yes, I can hear the nightingale,
  who killed her own child,
  how from her bloody chamber
  by the Simois she sings her cares,
  like a poet with a voice of many notes.
  Now the flocks pasture   540
  on Mount Ida, and I can hear the sounds
  of the shepherd's pipe sighing through the night.
  Sleep casts its spell on my eyes.
  For it comes sweetest to the lids near dawn.

FIRST CHORIST

  Why hasn't that scout come, the one
  Hector urged to spy on the ships?

SECOND CHORIST

  I'm worried. He's been gone a long time.

FIRST CHORIST

  Did he fall into a trap, then, and get himself killed?
  We'll soon know if there's cause for fear.

SECOND CHORIST

  I say we go call the Lycians to the fifth watch   550
  according to the order of our allotment.
  (*Chorus exits and Odysseus and Diomedes enter.*)

ODYSSEUS
    Diomedes, did you hear anything—the sound of fighting?
    Or do empty noises fall on my ears?

DIOMEDES
    It's nothing but the clanging irons
    of harnesses on the chariot rails.
    It gave me a scare, too, before I realized
    it was the racket from the harnessed horses.

ODYSSEUS
    Try not to run into their sentries in the dark.

DIOMEDES
    I'll watch my step even though it's pitch black.

ODYSSEUS
    If you wake one of them up, do you know their password?   560

DIOMEDES
    It's "Phoebus." I got it from Dolon.

ODYSSEUS
    Look at this!
    The enemy had made camp here.

DIOMEDES
    Yes, Dolon told us Hector would be sleeping here.
    I brought this spear along just for him.

ODYSSEUS
    So what does this mean? Has his troop gone somewhere else?

DIOMEDES
    Maybe he's trying to trick us?

ODYSSEUS

Why, Hector is bold now, bold since he has the upper hand.

DIOMEDES

What do we do then, Odysseus? We haven't found
the man asleep here. Our hopes are lost.   570

ODYSSEUS

Return as fast as we can to our anchored ships.
Whatever god gives him his success
is protecting him. Let's not push our luck.

DIOMEDES

Then let's go after Aeneas or the Trojan
we hate most, Paris, and cut off their heads.

ODYSSEUS

How in the dark, surrounded by a hostile army,
are you going to find and kill these two and get away?

DIOMEDES

Still, what a shame to return to the Argive ships
without doing any damage to the enemy.

ODYSSEUS

How can you say done nothing? Haven't we killed   580
that would-be spy on our ships and taken his spoils?
Do you plan to waste their entire encampment?

DIOMEDES

You're right, let's go back. And good luck to us.
(*Athena appears to the audience but not to Odysseus and Diomedes, who
only hear her voice.*)

ATHENA

Where are you two going? Withdrawing from the Trojan
position? Cut to the quick because the god
will not let you two kill Hector or Paris?

Haven't you heard about Rhesus, the man who
comes as Troy's ally in grand style?
Let him live through this night to sunrise,
and neither Achilles nor Ajax can prevent   590
him from destroying the entire Argive fleet.
He'll demolish your fortifications and create
widespread havoc inside your gates.
Kill him and you'll prevail. But leave Hector
to his sleep. Do not take off his head.
He will die—but by another's hand.

ODYSSEUS

Mistress Athena, I know your voice well
and your way of speaking. In all I do
you are always with me and protect me.
Tell us where he sleeps, this man to whom you direct us.   600
Where is he posted in the barbarian company?

ATHENA

He is nearby, apart from the main army,
sleeping outside the lines in a place
Hector gave him to stay till night passes into dawn.
Next to him the white horses for his Thracian chariot
are tethered, conspicuous in the darkness
like a swan's wing gleaming on the water.
Kill their master and lead them away,
an outstanding prize for your house. No place
on earth holds a team of horses like these.   610

ODYSSEUS

Diomedes, you can kill the Thracian men—
or leave them to me while you take care of the horses.

DIOMEDES

Leave the killing to me. You handle the horses.
You are the master of craft and deceit.
A man should be assigned where he does most good.

ATHENA

> Look at this, Alexander comes this way.
> He's probably heard from some guard
> a vague report of enemies in the area.

DIOMEDES

> Is he alone, or does he come with others?

ATHENA

> Alone. He seems headed for Hector's resting place   620
> to report spies have infiltrated the army.

DIOMEDES

> So then shouldn't he be the first to die?

ATHENA

> No, you will not overreach your fate.
> You do not have permission to kill him.
> But go quickly to those you are destined to slaughter.
> I will appear to Paris as his friend Cypris.
> I'll engage this hated man with lies
> and pretend to help him in his deeds.
> I have spoken. Even though he is in front of us,
> he will know and hear nothing of what will happen to him.   630

(Odysseus and Diomedes exit, and Paris [Alexander] enters.)

PARIS

> Hector? Brother? General?
> Are you asleep? Shouldn't you be waking up?
> An enemy has stolen into our encampment.
> Someone has come either to rob us or to spy on us.

ATHENA

> Don't be afraid. I, gentle Aphrodite, watch over you.
> I have some care for your war. And I remember
> your reverence and thank you for your kindness.
> Now in this moment of the Trojan army's prosperity,

I bring you a man and mighty friend,
the Thracian child of the music-making goddess.   640
The Muse is his mother and his father's name is River Strymon.

PARIS

You have always proved yourself well-disposed to me
and to Troy. When I chose in your favor,
I gained life's greatest treasure for my city.
I come because of vague rumors—a story
spreading among the sentries—that Achaean
spies are around. One says he hasn't seen anything.
Another nothing more than that he saw them.
That's why I'm here in Hector's camp.

ATHENA

You've nothing to fear. There is no trouble in the camp.   650
Hector has gone to assign the Thracians sleeping quarters.

PARIS

That's reassuring. I believe what you say
and go unafraid to take up my post.

ATHENA

Go now. Be sure I have your concerns in mind
and that I mean to see my friends succeed.
Yes, you will find out just how much I care for you.
(Paris exits and Athena calls out to Odysseus and Diomedes.)
Over here, you two. You're much too daring.
Laertes' son, give your sharp-edged sword a rest.
Our Thracian commander has fallen.
We've taken his horses. But the enemy know it   660
and are closing on you. Now hurry up
and run to the moored ships. Why do you hesitate
to save your lives when the enemy's all over the place?
*(Odysseus and Diomedes enter with the Chorus in pursuit as Athena
fades from view.)*

CHORUS
> Yo! Hey!
> Get them. Hit them. There. Yo!

FIRST CHORIST
> Who's this man?
> Take a look—at him, I say!

SECOND CHORIST
> This way everybody, this way.
> I've got them, I've grabbed hold of the thieves.

FIRST CHORIST
> You who stir up the army in the dark,   670
> what's your troop? Who are you? What country?

ODYSSEUS
> Nothing to you.

FIRST CHORIST
>   You'll die for the evil you've done this day.
> Quick, give me the password before my spear greets your chest!

ODYSSEUS
> Look, there's nothing to fear.

SECOND CHORIST
>   Over here! Get him, everybody.
> Did you kill Rhesus?

ODYSSEUS
>   No. But you could be the killer. Back off!

FIRST CHORIST
> We will not.

ODYSSEUS

> Hey! You mustn't kill a friend.

FIRST CHORIST

And so what's the password?

ODYSSEUS

> Phoebus.

SECOND CHORIST

> Right. Put up your spears.

Do you know where those men went?

ODYSSEUS

> They went that way.

FIRST CHORIST

After them everyone! Or should we sound the alarm?
No, wait! Let's not startle our allies in the night.   680
(Odysseus and Diomedes slip away.)

CHORUS

> *Strophe*

> What man was just here?
> Who will brag about the nerve he showed
> in slipping out of my grasp?
> Where can I find him now?
> To whom shall I compare him,
> this one who stepped without fear in the dark
> through our lines and guarded positions?
> Is he a Thessalian? Or maybe
> an inhabitant of a city on the Locrian coast?
> An islander who plunders the Sporades?   690
> Who is he? Where's he from? What country?
> Who is the highest god he prays to?

FIRST CHORIST

So was this or wasn't it Odysseus' work?
Judging from the past, it must be his.

SECOND CHORIST

Do you think so?

FIRST CHORIST

How can I not?

SECOND CHORIST

For sure, he's been bold with us.

FIRST CHORIST

Whose courage are you praising?

SECOND CHORIST

Odysseus'.

FIRST CHORIST

Don't praise that thief, that dirty fighter.

CHORUS

Antistrophe

He came once before
into our city with eyes running,   70
all wrapped up in rags,
his hand on a sword
hidden beneath his cloak.
Asking for bread, he shuffled like a slavish beggar,
squalid and with a filthy head.
He slandered the royal house of Atreus
up and down in so many ways
you'd think he was those war lords' enemy.
He deserves to be dead—he should have died
before he ever invaded Phrygia's shore.   71

FIRST CHORIST
Odysseus or not, I'm frightened.
Since we are on watch, Hector will blame us.

SECOND CHORIST
Blame us? For what?

FIRST CHORIST
For letting him down . . .

SECOND CHORIST
What did we do? What are you worried about?

FIRST CHORIST
Because they passed through us . . .

SECOND CHORIST
Who? Who did?

FIRST CHORIST
The men who invaded the Phrygian camp tonight.

CHARIOTEER *(offstage)*
My god, what terrible luck! No, no, oh, no!

FIRST CHORIST
Hey, listen! Quiet, keep down.
Maybe someone's coming into our trap.

CHARIOTEER *(still offstage)*
Help, help!   720
What a disaster for us Thracians.

SECOND CHORIST
This is an ally crying out.

CHARIOTEER *(entering)*

> Help! What bad luck for me and you, my Thracian chief.
> What a hateful sight Troy has been.
> What a way to end your life!

FIRST CHORIST

> Which of our allies are you? My eyes are dimmed,
> and I can't make you out in this darkness.

CHARIOTEER

> Where can I find a Trojan leader?
> Where's Hector spending the night
> sleeping under his shield?
> Who is in charge of this army? I want to report   730
> what we've suffered, what's been done to us
> by someone who's gone and disappeared
> but left a clear picture of the damage he's done.

SECOND CHORIST

> By what I gather from this man's words,
> something awful has happened to the Thracian force.

CHARIOTEER

> Our army has been wiped out, our king brought down
> by a treacherous blow. And oh, oh,
> my own bloody deep wound hurts so bad.
> Why couldn't I just die?
> Must Rhesus and I both be ingloriously killed   740
> in this Troy we came to help?

FIRST CHORIST

> This is no riddle. What he reports is evil.
> It's clear from what he says friends have perished.

CHARIOTEER

> What has happened is evil and more than evil—
> a disgrace. And this doubles the evil done.

For to die with glory, if one must die,
is still painful, I think, to him who dies—how not?—
yet it exalts his family and glorifies his house.
But we die without honor or purpose.
When Hector pointed out our sleeping quarters   750
and told us the password, we lay down
exhausted by our march. We didn't set
a night-long watch over the army, didn't stack
our shields in order, and didn't hang the whips
from the horses' yokes, since our king had been advised
you ruled the field and camped beside the Greek ships' cables.
Without a care we threw ourselves down and slept.
But my anxious heart awoke me.
Preparing to harness the horses for battle at dawn,
I was giving them as much fodder as I could.   760
Then I spotted two men prowling through our camp
in the pitch dark. As soon as I moved
they froze and backed off again.
I shouted at them to keep away from our camp.
I thought thieves had come from among our allies.
They said nothing, and I did nothing more.
I returned to my place and slept again.
But in my sleep a vision came to me.
The horses that I raised and drove
standing at Rhesus' side, I saw, as in a dream.   770
Wolves had mounted them and were riding on their backs.
The wolves whipped the horses' flanks with their tails,
driving them on. The horses bucked and snorted
wildly, terrified, and tossed their manes.
I roused as I warded those wild beasts
off the horses, awakened by my own nightmare.
Then, as I raised my head, I heard a man dying.
It was right beside me, my murdered master's hard death.
His new-shed blood, hot and spurting, splashed me.
I leaped up but had no spear in my hand.   780
As I groped and looked for a weapon,
a powerful man nearby stabbed me with his sword.

I felt the blade go in, between my ribs,
a deep, staggering wound.
I fell face down. The two men stole the car
and team of horses and escaped.
(*groans in pain*)
    The pain is killing me, I can't stand up.
    I know it's a disaster. I saw it.
    Still, I can't figure out how these men died
    or who did it. But I can make a guess—   79(
    I think it was "friends" who did this terrible thing.

FIRST CHORIST
    Driver for that luckless Thracian king,
    no one but an enemy could have done this.
    Look, Hector himself comes. He has learned
    about this calamity and shares your grief, I'm sure.

HECTOR
    How could these deadly raiders,
    these enemy spies,
    get past you—a disgrace—and slaughter an army
    without your confronting them coming in
    or going out? Who but you will pay for this?   80(
    It was your job to guard our forces.
    They're gone without a scratch, full of jeers
    for fainthearted Phrygians and their leader, me.
    Now get this message—I swear by my father Zeus—
    you'll get death either by the lash
    or beheading for this work, or take me,
    Hector, for a coward or a nobody.

CHORUS

            Antistrophe

    Ah no, no!
    It was to a great lord and protector
    that we came when we arrived   81(

with news of their lighting fires near their ships.
From that moment, we swear by the springs of Simois,
we have not slept, nor our eyes drooped once.
Don't be angry with us, dear lord.
We are guiltless in all of this affair.
If in time any unseemly deed
or word you find in us, give the order
to bury us alive in this ground. We won't appeal it.

CHARIOTEER

We're all barbarian here. Why do you threaten them
and try to subvert my judgment with twisted words?   820
This was your doing. We, the dead and walking wounded,
know whom to hold responsible—you alone.
It would take a long and clever speech
to persuade me you didn't murder your friends
and steal their horses. It was for them you killed
the allies whom you had pressed so hard to come.
They came and they're dead. Paris showed more class than you
when he disgraced hospitality, you, you friend-killer.
And don't try to tell me some Argive came and murdered us.
Who could have evaded the Trojan lines   830
and reached us without being seen?
You and the Phrygian army were set before us.
Which of all your allies was wounded
or killed when these so-called enemies came?
We are the casualties, the wounded and some,
worse-off, who will never again see the light of day.
It's plain. We accuse no Argive of this.
Who could slip by enemies in the night
and find Rhesus' bed on the ground—unless
a god directed the killers? They had no idea   840
he had even come. No, this is your scheme.

HECTOR

I have had experience with allied forces
for as long as the Achaeans have been in our land.

To date, I've not heard one complaint from them.
So why I should start with you? I would never
allow the love of horses to lead me to kill my friends.
This sounds more like Odysseus. Who but that man
among the Argives could have planned and done this?
Him I fear, and I'm also very worried
that he might have crossed paths with Dolon and killed him.   850
He's been gone a long time and hasn't shown up.

CHARIOTEER

I have no idea who this Odysseus is.
And it was not an enemy who hurt us.

HECTOR

Go ahead and think so, since you won't change your mind.

CHARIOTEER

O land of my fathers, why can't I die in you?

HECTOR

Don't die! This pile of dead bodies is enough.

CHARIOTEER

Where shall I turn now that I've lost my leader?

HECTOR

In my own house we will shelter and heal you.

CHARIOTEER

How shall a murderer's hands nurse me?

HECTOR

The man just can't stop telling the same story.   860

CHARIOTEER

Death to the killer! But since my tongue is not aimed
at you, save your big words. Justice will take care of it.

HECTOR
>Pick him up. Carry him into my house.
>Care for him so he'll have no cause for complaint.
>And you, go to those upon the wall,
>to Priam and the elders, and urge them
>to bury the dead beside the fork in the highway.

(Two or three Trojans, not members of the Chorus, carry off the
>>>*Charioteer, while another leaves to deliver Hector's*
>>>*message.)*

CHORUS
>Can it be that Troy's great success has been reversed?
>Does the god once again bring us new troubles?
>What does he hold in store for us?   870

(The Muse, with Rhesus in her arms, appears above.)
>But look, look over there,
>my King, above your head! What god is sent,
>making a litter of her arms
>for a newly dead man?
>It's terrifying to look upon this apparition.

MUSE
>Step up and look at me, Trojans.
>I, the Muse, one of the sisters revered by the wise,
>stand before you. Having seen my dear son
>pitifully slain by the enemy. In time the killer,
>that crafty Odysseus, will be brought to justice.   880

>>*Strophe*

>Now I make a new song of grief.
>I mourn for you, son, mourn, Oh,
>what pain you gave your mother
>that luckless, black day
>you set out for Troy.
>You defied us. Against my restraints,

despite your father's pleas, you went.
I cry, oh, me for you, O dearest,
sweetest head, my child, oh, me.

CHORUS

    I feel for you and grieve for your son   890
    as much as possible for one who is not kin.

MUSE

      Strophe

Death to Diomedes, son of Oeneus.
Death to Odysseus, Laertes' son,
who made me childless
who had the best child of all.
And death to her who abandoned
her Greek home to lie in a Phrygian bed.
She destroyed you, my dearest,
and for Troy's sake, emptied countless
cities of good, brave men.   900
How often during your lifetime and now from Hades,
O Thamyris, Philammon's son, have you scorched my heart.
Your insolence defeated you, and your strife with the Muses
made me give birth to this unfortunate son.
O son, as I waded through the river's current
Strymon pulled me to his bed where I conceived you.
That was when we Muses, decked out with instruments,
came to the gold-flecked earth of Pangaeus' crag.
We had come for the great musical contest
with the master singer of Thrace and we blinded   910
Thamyris, who had so often mocked our skill.
After I had given birth to you, I was ashamed
before my sisters. For my lost virginity, I threw you back
into your father's teeming waters, and Strymon gave you
not into the care of mortal hands but to the maidens of his
          springs.

There the nymphs raised you beautifully,
and you ruled over Thrace, the first of men, my son.
As long as you stayed home, defending it
with bloodthirsty courage, I had no fear you would die.
Still I warned you against ever going to Troy,   920
knowing your fate there. But Hector's constant
embassies and the elders' countless appeals
convinced you to go to the aid of friends.
Athena, you alone are responsible for this death—
neither Odysseus nor Diomedes could have done a thing
if you hadn't enabled it—don't think this escapes me.
Yet we sister Muses especially honor
your city by our presence in Athens.
And Orpheus, the very cousin of this dead man
whom you have killed, enlightened Athens   930
through mysteries and revelations. Musaeus, too,
him we sisters and Phoebus taught, your most respected
citizen and foremost poet among men.
And this is my reward, to hold my son in my arms
and to wail. I will give you no more artists.

CHORUS

So, Hector, the Thracian charioteer reproached
us wrongly for plotting Rhesus' death.

HECTOR

I knew it. It didn't take an oracle's words
to see that Odysseus' tricks caused this death.
And I, when I saw the Greek army camped   940
on our shores, how could I not send my heralds
to our allies to ask them to come help our country?
I sent them. And, obliged to me, the man came to help.
In no way do I rejoice in his death.
I am prepared to build him a tomb
and to burn the splendor of countless robes for him.
He came as a friend and departs a luckless thing.

MUSE

He shall not descend to the black country below.
This much I will seek from the infernal bride,
Demeter's daughter, the goddess of harvests,   950
that she release his soul. She owes it to me
to show she still honors Orpheus' kin.
But for me he will henceforth be like a dead man
who sees the light no more. Who will never
return, and never again see his living mother.
Hidden in caves of silver-veined earth
he will lie, living on as a deified man.
As Bacchus' prophet, taking Pangaeus' rock
as his home, he will be revered as a god by the initiate.
The pain of the sea goddess I will bear   960
more easily now, for her son must also die.
First, my son, we sisters will sing dirges for you,
then for Achilles on Thetis' day of sorrow.
Pallas Athena, who killed you, cannot save him.
The arrow meant for him waits in Apollo's quiver.
O disastrous childbearing, humanity's grief!
Whoever can reckon the good from the bad,
will choose to live childless, never to bear children to the grave.

(Muse disappears.)

CHORUS

Rhesus' funeral is his mother's concern now.
But if you want to do the work you've planned,   970
Hector, it is time. The new day dawns.

HECTOR

Go, tell the allies to arm directly
and to harness the necks of their chariot teams.
Then, torches in hand, let them await the cry
of the Etruscan trumpet. I am confident
we can overrun the Achaean trench and walls,

set their ships on fire, and bring Troy her day of liberation
with the approaching rays of the sun.

CHORUS
Trust in the King. Let's march, well-armed
and disciplined, and pass all this on   980
to those who fight with us. If the god on our side
allows it, we just might win.

Stressed syllables are marked. The descriptions below are based primarily on the Oxford Classical Dictionary.

Acastus (a-kas'-tus). Son of Pelias, brother of Alcestis.

Achaeans (a-kee'-ans). Race of warlike bronze-age people who, with the Ionians, came into Greece from the north in the second millennium B.C. Achaea and Achaeans are often used as synonyms for Greece and the Greeks.

Achelous (a-kel'-oh-us). God of the river of the same name in Epirus.

Achilles (a-kil'-eez). Son of Peleus and Thetis, the best of the Greek warriors at Troy, and hero of the *Iliad*.

Admetus (ad-meet'-us). King of Pherae and husband of Alcestis.

Adrastus (a-dras'-tus). King of Argos, one of the Seven against Thebes.

Adrasteia (ad-ras-tye'-a). Plain below Mount Ida, near Troy.

Aeacus (ee'-a-cus). King of the island of Oeopia, where, after a plague destroyed all his subjects, Zeus repopulated the kingdom by turning ants into human beings.

Aegina (ee-jee'-na). Island in the Aegean Sea.

Aegisthus (ee-gis'-thus). Son of Thyestes, therefore a cousin of Agamemnon and Menelaus. Clytemnestra's lover.

Aeneas (a-nee'-us). Trojan leader, son of Anchises and Aphrodite.

Aenia (ee'-nya). City in Macedonia.

Aetolia (ee-tol'-i-a). Country in the middle of Greece of which Tydeus was king.

Agamemnon (ag-a-mem'-non). King of Mycenae, husband of Clytemnestra, and brother of Menelaus, king of Sparta. They were sons of Pleisthenes the son of Atreus (or, in some versions, they were themselves sons of Atreus).

Agenor (a-jee'-nor). King of Phoenicia, father of Cadmus.

Ajax (ay'-jaks). Son of Telamon king of Salamis, brother of Teucer. One c
the great warriors at Troy.

Ajax (2). Son of Oileus, leader of Locrian contingent to Troy.

Alcestis (al-ses'-tis). Wife of Admetus king of Thessaly, in whose place sh
is willing to die but is saved by Heracles.

Alcmene (alk-may'-nay). Daughter of Electryon, mother of Heracles b
Zeus, who appeared in her husband Amphitryon's shape.

Alexander. Name for Paris.

Alpheus (al'-fee-us). River in the Peloponnese.

Ammon (am'-on). Chief Egyptian deity, associated with Thebes.

Amphiaraus (am-fee-a-ray'-us). One of the Seven against Thebes.

Amphion (am'-fee-on). Son of Zeus and Antiope; with his brother Zethu
founder of Thebes.

Amyclae (am'-i-klye). Achaean center on the bank of the Eurotas Rive
south of Sparta.

Andromache (an-drom'-a-kee). Wife of Hector and mother of Astyanax
After Hector died, she married his brother Helenus. Bore Molos
sus to Neoptolemus.

Antigone (an-tig'-o-nee). Daughter of Oedipus and Jocasta, sister of Eteo
cles, Polynices, and Ismene.

Aphrodite (af-ro-dye'-tee). Latin Venus. Goddess of love.

Apidanus (ap-i-dan'-us). Large river in Thessaly.

Apollo (a-pol'-ow). God of music, healing, and prophecy. Son of Zeus an
Leto, twin brother of Artemis.

Archelaus (ar-kel-ow'-us). King of Macedonia, patron of Euripides.

Ares (air'-ez). Latin Mars. God of war.

Arethusa (ar-e-thu'-za). Nymph who was turned into a fountain nea
Syracuse.

Argo (ar'-go). Jason's ship. His companions on his quest for the Golde
Fleece were called the Argonauts.

Argos (ar'-gos). Strictly speaking, an ancient city, the capital of Argolis i
the Peloponnese. But all the inhabitants of the Peloponnese, an
even all the Greeks, are called Argives.

Aristaeus (a-ris-tay'-us). Son of Apollo and the nymph Cyrene. He marrie
Autonoë; their son was Actaeon the famous hunter.

Artemis (ar'-te-mis). Latin Diana. Virgin goddess of hunting, prophecy, an
childbirth. Daughter of Zeus and Leto, elder twin sister of Apollo

Asclepius (as-klep'-i-us). God of medicine.

Asopus (a-so'-pus). River in Thessaly.

Astyanax (as-tee'-a-naks). Young son of Hector and Andromache, killed at the fall of Troy. His name means "lord of the citadel."

Atalanta (a-ta-lan'-ta). Virgin huntress, companion of Artemis. Promised to marry someone who could defeat her in a footrace; mother of Parthenopaeus.

Athena (a-thee'-na). Latin Minerva. Goddess of wisdom and patroness of Athens.

Atlas (at'-las). Titan, son of Iapetus and brother of Prometheus. Traditionally held the world on his shoulders.

Atreus (ay'-tree-us). Son of Pelops, father of Agamemnon and Menelaus, brother of Thyestes, whom he caused to eat the flesh of his own sons. (Or in some versions, he was the father of Pleisthenes and grandfather of Agamemnon and Menelaus.)

Attica (at'-i-ca). Area around Athens.

Aulis (owl'-is). Port in Boeotia where the Greek fleet gathered. The site of the sacrifice of Iphigenia.

Autonoë (au-ton'-oh-ee). Daughter of Cadmus who married Aristaeus, by whom she had Actaeon.

Bacchus (bak'-us). God of wine and drinking, son of Zeus and Semele. The Bacchanalia were his festivals.

Bacchantes (bak-kan'-teez). Also called Bacchae, the priestesses of Bacchus.

Bistonia (bis-toh'-ni-a). Area in Thrace, home of Diomedes (2).

Boeotia (bee-oh'-sha). District in eastern Greece.

Cadmus (kad'-mus). Son of Agenor and sister of Europa. He established the country called Boeotia and founded the city of Thebes, which he populated with men (Spartoi) who sprang from the teeth of a dragon he had killed. He married Harmonia, and introduced the alphabet into Greece.

Calchas (kal'-kus). Soothsayer who accompanied the Greeks, and who told Agamemnon at Aulis that he must sacrifice his daughter Iphigenia.

Capaneus (ka-pa-nay'-us). One of the Seven against Thebes.

Carneius (kar-nay'-us). Name for Apollo. The Carnea was the main Dorian festival.

Cassandra (ka-san'-dra). Daughter of Priam and Hecuba who was loved by Apollo. He gave her the gift of clairvoyance, but ruined the gift my wetting her lips with his tongue so that no one would ever believe her predictions.

Castalia (kas-tay'-lya). Spring near Delphi.

Castor (kas'-tor). Son of Leda, brother of Pollux. The two are called the Dioscuri.

Cecrops (see'-crops). Legendary founder of Athens.

Centaurs (sen'-taurz). Creatures who were half human and half horse; lived in Thessaly.

Chalcis (kal'-kis). Chief city of Euboea, controlling the Euripus channel.

Charon (shar'-on). Ferryman of dead souls across the river Styx to Hades.

Charybdis (ka-rib'-dis). Whirlpool supposedly in a strait opposite Scylla.

Chiron (kye'-ron). Centaur who was wounded in the knee by a poisoned arrow of Heracles. The pain was so excruciating he begged Zeus to deprive him of his immortality so he could die. He was placed among the constellations and became Sagitarius.

Cilicia (sil-is'-ya). District in southern Asia Minor.

Circe (ser'-see; Greek Kir'-kee). Sorceress, daughter of Helios and the Oceanid Perse.

Cithaeron (ki-thy'-ron). Mountain in Boeotia sacred to Zeus and the Muses.

Clytemnestra (kly-tem-nes'-tra). Daughter of Leda, sister of Helen, wife of Agamemnon, mistress of Aegisthus, and mother of Iphigenia, Orestes, and Electra.

Cocytus (ko-kee'-tus). River in Hades.

Colonus (ka-lo'-nus). Area in Attica north of the Acropolis.

Corinth (kor'-inth). City of Greece on the Isthmus of Corinth.

Coroebus (kor-ee'-bus). Son of Mygdon, Phrygian leader.

Corycus (kor'-i-kus). Mountain in Asia Minor, now called Curco.

Creon (kray'-on). Brother of Jocasta and king of Thebes after the death of Polynices and Eteocles.

Cronus (kro'-nus). Latin Saturn. Titan, son of Heaven (Uranus) and Earth (Gaia). He married his sister Rhea; their children included Demeter, Hades, Hera, Hestia, Poseidon, and Zeus, who overthrew him.

Cyclopes (sy-klop'-eez). Race of giants who had one eye in the middle of their foreheads. Polyphemus was chief among them.

Cycnus (sik'-nus). Son of Ares who robbed travelers bringing offerings to Delphi; killed by Heracles and Iolaus.

Cypris (kip'-ris). Name for Aphrodite.

Danaë (da'-na-ay). Daughter of Acrisius king of Argos and Eurydice. Mother of Perseus by Zeus who visited her as a shower of gold.

Dardanus (dar'-da-nus). Ancestor of the Trojan kings.

Deiphobus (de-i-foh'-bus). Son of Priam and Hecuba. According to later authors, he married Helen after the death of Paris.

Delos (del'-os). One of the Cyclades north of Naxos, island where Leto gave birth to Apollo and Artemis.

Delphi (del'-fye). Town on the southwest side of Mount Parnassus where the Pythia gave oracular messages inspired by Apollo.

Demeter (de-meet'-er). Latin Ceres. Earth-mother goddess of grains and harvests. Her daughter was Persephone.

Diomedes (di-o-meed'-eez). Son of Tydeus, one of the bravest of the Greeks at the Trojan War.

Diomedes (2). Son of Ares and Cyrene, king in Thrace, owner of a team of man-eating horses which Heracles drove back to Greece.

Dionysus (di-o-nee'-sus). Another name for Bacchus. The Dionysia was the wine festival in the god's honor.

Dioscuri (dee-o-skur'-eye). The twins Castor and Pollus. Served as divine messengers.

Dirce (dir'-see). Second wife of Lycus, king of Thebes. He married her after divorcing Antiope. After the divorce, Antiope became pregnant by Zeus, and Dirce, suspecting Lycus was the father, imprisoned and tormented Antiope, who nonetheless escaped and bore Amphion and Zethus on Mount Cithaeron.

Dodona (do-doh'-na). Town in Epirus (some say Thessaly) where there was a temple to Zeus and the most ancient oracle of Greece. There was a grove of sacred oak trees surrounding the temple.

Dolon (doh'-lon). Trojan spy.

Echinea (e-kin'-i-a). Small isthmus near the mouth of the Achelous.

Electra (e-lek'-tra). Daughter of Agamemnon and Clytemnestra, sister of Orestes.

Elis (el'-is). Plain in the northwest Peloponnese.

Epaphus (e-pa'-fus). Son of Zeus and Io who founded Memphis, where he was worshiped as a god.

Epeia (e-pye'-a). Region in the Peloponnese.

Erechtheus (e-rek'-thee-us). Son of Pandion and sixth king of Athens.

Eros (air'-os). Latin Cupid. God of love.

Eteocles (e-tee'-o-cleez). Son of Oedipus and Jocasta, brother of Polynice

Eteoclus (e-tee-oh'-clus). Son of Iphis, one of the Seven against Thebes.

Etruscans. Civilization of Italy, between the Tridentine Alps and the Gulf c
    Salerno.

Euboea (you-bee'-a). The long island that stretches from the Gulf of Paga
    sae to Andros, the chief cities of which were Chalcis and Eretri;

Eumelus (you-may'-lus). Son of Admetus.

Eumolpus (you-mol'-pus). Son of Poseidon, ruler of Eleusis.

Europa (you-roh'-pa). Daughter of Agenor king of Phoenicia, mother c
    Minos, Rhadamanthus, and Sarpedon by Zeus, who in the form c
    a bull carried her off.

Euripus (you-rip'-us). Strait that separates the island of Euboea from th
    coast of Boeotia.

Eurotas (eu-roh'-tus). River near Sparta that the Spartans worshiped as
    powerful god.

Eurystheus (you-ris'-thee-us). Son of Sthenelus and Nicippe, king of Ti
    ryns. Heracles was enslaved to him while he performed the Twelv
    Labors.

Eurytus (you'-ri-tus). King of Oechalia and father of Iole, whom Heracle
    killed.

Euxine Sea. The Black Sea.

Ganymede (gan'-i-meed). Brother of Priam and cupbearer of Zeus.

Gerenia (ger-een'-i-a). Mountain near Corinth.

Gorgons. Three monstrous sisters with golden wings and hair entwine
    with serpents. Medusa, the only mortal one, is the best known.

Gouneus (goo-nay'-us). Father of Laonome who was Heracles' mistress.

Hades (hay'-deez). Latin Pluto. The world of the dead, or the god wh
    ruled it.

Haemon (hy'-mon). Son of Creon king of Thebes. Killed himself on dis
    covering Antigone's suicide.

Harmonia (har-mon-ee'-a). Daughter of Ares and Aphrodite, married Cad
    mus. Sometimes called Hermione.

Hecate (he'-ka-te or hek'-at). Goddess who presided over magic and witch
    craft. Often conflated with Persephone and Artemis.

Hector (hek'-tor). Son of Priam and Hecuba, and the chief warrior of Troy
    He married Andromache.

Hecuba (hek′-you-ba). Wife of Priam, mother of Hector, Paris, Helenus, Polydorus, Cassandra, Polyxena, and a number of other children.

Helen (hel′-en). Daughter of Leda, sister of Clytemnestra, wife of Menelaus, taken by Paris to Troy.

Helenus (hel′-en-us). Son of Priam and Hecuba, a soothsayer. He married Andromache, widow of his brother Hector.

Hellas (hel′-as). Name originally applied to a territory and a small tribe in southern Thessaly, it later came to include all Greeks.

Hephaestus (hef-fes′-tus). Latin Vulcan. God of fire and smithing.

Hera (her′-a). Latin Juno. Wife and sister of Zeus, and queen of heaven.

Heracles (her′-a-kleez). Latin Hercules. Son of Zeus by Alcmena. He was tormented by Hera and made to perform many arduous labors.

Hermes (her′-meez). Latin Mercury. Son of Zeus and Maia. He was the messenger god and patron of messengers and merchants.

Hermione (her-my′-o-nee). Daughter of Menelaus and Helen. She was married to Neoptolemus but had no children by him. Eventually she married Orestes and had a son Tisamenus.

Hippomedon (hip-pom′-e-don). One of the Seven against Thebes.

Homole (ho′-mo-lay). Mountain in Thessaly.

Hydra (hye′-dra). Monster that lived in lake Lerna in the Peloponnese. It had a hundred heads, and as soon as one was cut off two more grew from the wound.

Ida (eye′-da). Mountain near Troy; more properly, the whole ridge of mountains that are the source of the Simois, Scamander, Aesopus, and other rivers.

Ilium (il′-i-um) or Ilion. Name for Troy.

Io (eye′-o). Daughter of Inachus. Loved by Zeus and turned by him into a white cow to conceal his adultery from Hera.

Iolcas (eye′-ol-kus). Town in Thessaly.

Iphigenia (if-i-jen-eye′-a). Daughter of Agamemnon and Clytemnestra whom he sacrificed at Aulis.

Iphis (if′-is). King of Argos and adviser to Polynices.

Ismene (iz-may′-nay). Sister of Antigone, Polynices, and Eteocles.

Ixion (iks′-ee-on). King of Thessaly. He offended Zeus by trying to rape Hera and was punished by being bound on a wheel that spins eternally.

Jocasta (jo-cas'-ta). Mother and wife of Oedipus, daughter of Menoeceus, sister of Creon.

Kore (kor'-e). Greek word for "maiden," often used as a name for Persephone or Athena.

Labdacus (lab'-da-cus). Father of Laius who was father of Oedipus.

Laconia. District of southern Greece of which Sparta was the capital.

Laertes (lay-air'-tees). Father of Odysseus.

Laius (lay'-us). Father of Oedipus.

Laomedon (lay-om'-e-don). King of Troy, father of Priam.

Leda (lee'-da). Wife of king Tyndareus of Sparta, mother of Helen, Clytemnestra, Castor, and Pollux.

Leitus (lye'-tus). Boeetian commander at Troy.

Lemnos (lem'-nos). Island in the Aegean Sea sacred to Hephaestus, now called Stalimine.

Lerna (ler'-na). Country in the Argolid where Heracles killed the Hydra.

Liguria (ly-gur'-ya). Area along the Italian coast from the Rhône to the Arno rivers.

Locris (lok'-ris). Region in central Greece.

Loxias (lok'-see-us). Name for Apollo.

Lycaoön (lik'-a-ohn). Son of Ares

Lycia (lish'-ya). Mountainous country in southwest Asia Minor.

Lydia (lid'-i-a). Kingdom of Asia Minor.

Maenads (mee'-nads). The Bacchantes.

Maia (mye'-a). One of the Pleiades, mother of Hermes by Zeus.

Mecistes (me-kis'-teez) or Mecisteus (me-kis'-te-us). Son of Echion and companion to Ajax.

Menelaus (me-ne-lay'-us). King of Sparta, son of Atreus, brother of Agamemnon, husband of Helen.

Menoeceus (men-ee'-kee-us). Descendant of Echion, father of Creon and Jocasta

Meriones (mer'-i-o-neez). Idomeneus' charioteer at Troy, son of Ares.

Molossia (mo-los'-i-a). Country ruled by Molossus son of Andromache and Neoptolemus, famous for its dogs.

Musaeus (mu-say'-us). Mythical singer, associated with Eleusis or Thrace

Muses. Goddesses of the arts, centered at Pieria.

Mycenae (my-see'-nee). Town in the Peloponnese where Agamemnon ruled.

Myconos (mik'-o-nos). Island, one of the Cyclades.

Mygdon (mig'-don). Phrygian general, father of Coroebus.

Myrmidons (meer'-mi-donz). People of southwest Thessaly, said to have been descended from ants who had been changed to people.

Mysia (miz'-ya). Area near the Aegean Sea.

Nemesis (nem'-e-sis). Goddess of retribution; in some stories, mother of Helen by Zeus.

Nereus (nee'-ree-us). God of the sea who married Doris and with her had fifty daughters called the Nereids, who included Thetis and Psamathe.

Nestor (nes'-tor). Son of Neleus and Chloris, companion of Menelaus.

Niobe (nye'-o-bee). Daughter of Tantalus, wife of Amphion of Thebes. She boasted that she was superior to Leto because of her many children, whereupon Leto's children Apollo and Artemis killed Niobe's children. Her grief became legendary.

Odysseus (o-dis'-yus). Latin Ulysses. King of Ithaca and one of the Greek heroes of the Trojan war. His domestic situation with faithful Penelope awaiting his return is often contrasted with Agamemnon's difficulties.

Oedipus (ed'-i-pus). Son of Laius and Jocasta; husband of Jocasta, father of Antigone, Ismene, Polynices, and Eteocles.

Oeneus (ee'-nee-us). King of Calydon, father by Althaea of Meleager and Deianira.

Oenone (ee-noh'-nay). Nymph of Mt. Ida, loved and deserted by Paris.

Ogygia (o-ji'-jya). Name for Boeotia.

Oileus (oy'-le-us). King of the Locrians and father of Ajax.

Olympus (o-lim'-pus). Mountain of Thessaly so tall that the Greeks believed it touched the heavens; it was therefore the home of the Olympian gods.

Orestes (or-es'-teez). Son of Agamemnon and Clytemnestra, brother of Electra and Iphigenia.

Orpheus (or'-fee-us). Son of Apollo and a Muse (some say Calliope), who was so gifted with the lyre that even rivers stopped to listen to him.

Orythria (or-ith'-ri-a). Area in Thrace

Paeonia (pye'-on-ya). Region of Macedonia.

Palamedes (pal-a-mee'-deez). Clever hero, son of Nauplius and Clymene.

Pallas (pal'-us). Name for Athena.

Pan. God of shepherds and hunters. He had horns and goat feet and in vented the syrinx or reed flute.

Pangaeum (pan-gay'-um). Area around Mount Pangaeus in Thrace.

Panthous (pan'-thoos). Trojan priest of Apollo, father of Polydamas.

Paris (pair'-is). Also called Alexander. Son of Priam and Hecuba who ab ducted Helen from Sparta and caused the Trojan War.

Parnassus (par-nas'-us). Mountain in Phocis, sacred to the Muses.

Parthenopaeus (par-then-o-pye'-us). One of the Seven against Thebes.

Peleus (pee'-le-us). King of Thessaly, father of Achilles by Thetis.

Pelias (pee'-li-as). Son of Poseidon and Tyro and king of Iolcus. He mu dered Aeson, his half-brother.

Pelion (pee'-li-on). Mountain in Thessaly.

Pelops (pel'-ops). Son of Tantalus, who cut him up and served him to th Phrygian gods. Restored to life, obtained Hippodamia after de feating her father Oenomaus in a chariot race by trickery. Father o Atreus.

Pergamos (per'-ga-mos). City near Troy.

Persephone (per-sef'-o-nee). Latin Proserpine. Daughter of Demeter an queen of Hades.

Perseus (per'-see-us). Son of Zeus and Danaë, ancestor of Heracles. Kille the Gorgon Medusa.

Pherae (fair'-eye). City in Thessaly.

Pheres (feer'-eez). Father of Admetus

Philammon (phil'-a-mon). Legendary musician and poet, son of Apollo.

Phocis (foh'-kis). District of Greece next to Boeotia on the Gulf of Corinth

Phoebe (fee'-bee). Name given to Artemis as the moon goddess. daughte of Leda

Phoebus (fee'-bus). Name for Apollo.

Phoenicia (fo-nees'-ya). Land along the eastern Mediterranean coast from Syria to southern Lebanon.

Phrygia (fri'-jee-a). Country in Asia Minor in which Troy was the mos prominent city.

Phthia (fthy'-a). Birthplace of Achilles in Thessaly near Mt. Othrys.

Pleiades (plee'-a-des). Daughters of Atlas, of whom Maia was one.

Pollux (pol'-ux). Twin brother of Castor, also called Polydeuces. Se Dioscuri.

Polybus (pol'-i-bus). King of Corinth. He and his wife Merope, childless, adopted the infant Odysseus.

Polyclemenus (pol-i-klee'-me-nus). Son of Poseidon, defender of Thebes

Polydamas (pol-i-dam'-us). Son of Panthous, advisor to Hector.

Polydeuces (pol-i-doo'-seez). Alternate name for Pollux.

Polydorus (po-li-dor'-us). Youngest son of Priam and Hecuba, killed by his brother-in-law Polymestor.

Polynices (po-li-nye'-seez). Son of Oedipus and Jocasta, brother of Eteocles.

Polyphemus (po-le-fee'-mus). Chief of the Cyclopes.

Polyxena (po-lix-ee'-na). Daughter of Priam and Hecuba. After the war she was sacrified to Achilles' shade in a symbolic marriage.

Poseidon (po-sye'-don). Latin Neptune. God of the sea, brother of Demeter, Hades, Hera, Hestia, and Zeus.

Potniae (pot'-nee-eye). Town in Boeotia where Bacchus had a temple.

Priam (pry'-am). King of Troy, husband of Hecuba.

Prometheus (pro-mee'-thee-us). Son of the Titan Iapetus and the Oceanid Clymene. Stole fire from the gods, punished and imprisoned, eventually freed by Heracles.

Protesilaus (pro-tes-i-la'-us). Husband of Laodamia, leader of Thessalian contingent at Troy, first to be killed.

Pylos (pye'-los). City in Elis, Nestor's capital.

Pytho (pye'-tho). Ancient name of Delphi, called that because of the great serpent Apollo killed there.

Rhesus (ree'-sus). Thracian ally of Priam, son of the river Strymon and a Muse.

Salamis (sal'-a-mis). Island in the Saronic Gulf off Eleusis.

Sarpedon (sar-pee'-don). Son of Zeus and Laodamia, commander of the Lycian contingent of Priam's allies at Troy.

Scamander (ska-man'-der). River near Troy.

Scylla (sil'-a). Daughter of Nisus whom she betrayed for the love of Minos, king of Crete. When the latter spurned her, she threw herself into the sea and was transformed to rocks dangerous to sailors.

Scyros (sky'-ros). Island off Euboea.

Scythia (sith'-ee-a). General term for area north and east of Greece.

Semele (sem'-e-le). Daughter of Cadmus and Harmonia, and, by Zeus, the mother of Bacchus.

Simois (sim′-o-is). River near Troy.

Sirens (sye′-renz). Enchantresses who lived on an island near Scylla and Charybdis.

Sisyphus (sis′-i-fus). Sufferer in Hades condemned to roll a huge stone up a mountain, a task repeated endlessly.

Sparta (spar′-ta). Greek city-state in the Peloponnese.

Sphinx. Monster, part animal, part human, challenged by Odysseus.

Sporades (spor′-a-deez). Islands in the Aegean Sea.

Sthenelus (sthen′-e-lus). Tragic poet.

Strymon (strye′-mon). River between Thrace and Macedon, father of Rhesus.

Talthybius (tal-thi′-bi-us). Herald of the Greeks

Tantalus (tan′-ta-lus). King of Phrygia, son of Zeus, father of Pelops and Niobe.

Taphiae (taf′-ee-eye). Islands in the Ionian Sea.

Telamon (tel′-a-mon). King of Salamis and comrade of Heracles, father of Ajax and Teucer.

Telemachus (tel-e′-ma-kus). Son of Odysseus and Penelope, eventually married Circe.

Teumesus (too-mes′-us). Mountain in Boeotia and the nearby village.

Thamyris (tham-eye′-rus). Thracian bard, son of Philammon, blinded by the Muses for boasting he would win a contest even if they opposed him.

Thebes (theebz). City in Boeotia.

Theseus (thee′-see-us). Son of Aegeus and Aethra and king of Athens.

Thesprotia (thes-pro′-sha). Area of southwest Epirus, extending to Dodona.

Thessaly (thes′-a-lee). Territory to the north of Greece proper.

Thestius (thes′-ti-us). King of Pleuron in Aetolia, father of Leda.

Thetis (thee′-tis). Nereid, wife of Peleus, mother of Achilles.

Thrace (thrays). Area encompassing most of the world north of the Black Sea.

Thronium (throh′-ni-um). Town in Phocis.

Thymbraeus (thim-brye′-us). Name for Apollo.

Tiresias (ti-rees′-i-us). Great prophet of Thebes who was turned into a woman and then back to a man. He was blinded by Athena because he caught sight of her bathing.

Tiryns (teer′-inz). Center on the Argive plain, ruled by Eurystheus.

Titans. Legendary predecessors of the gods.

Tydeus (tid'-ee-us). One of the Seven against Thebes.

Tyndareus (tin-dar'-i-us). King of Laconia and husband of Leda.

Tyre. City in southern Phoenicia.

Xenios (ksen'-yos). Epithet for Zeus calling attention to his special interest in the sacred host-guest relationship.

Zethus (zeth'-us) or Zetus (zet'-us). Son of zeus and Antiope and brother of Amphion, with whom he built Thebes.

Zeus (zoos). Latin Jupiter. Son of the Titans Cronus and Rhea, brother of Demeter, Hades, Hera (whom he married), Hestia, and Poseidon. After he overthrew Cronus he became the chief Greek god.

About the Translators

FRED CHAPPELL, a North Carolina native, was educated at Duke University and has taught literature and writing for three decades at the University of North Carolina at Greensboro. He has published nearly twenty-five books, and has received a Rockefeller Grant and the Best Foreign Novel prize from the Académie Français, as well as the Bollingen Prize.

GEORGE ECONOMOU received his Ph.D. degree from Columbia University and has taught English at the University of Oklahoma since 1983. He is the author of several volumes of poetry, including *Landed Natures, Ameriki: Book One and Selected Earlier Poems*, and *harmonies & fits*, as well as the critical book *The Goddess Natura in Medieval Literature* and the verse translation *William Langland's* Piers Plowman: *The C Version* (University of Pennsylvania Press). He has received fellowships from the American Council of Learned Societies, the National Endowment for the Arts, and the Rockefeller Foundation.

RICHARD ELMAN was the author of twenty-six books of fiction, poetry, and journalism, including *An Education in Blood, Tar Beach, Homage to Fats Navarro, Disco Frito, Cocktails at Somoza's*, and the novelization of the movie *Taxi Driver*. He published widely in magazines and quarterlies and broadcast reviews and commentary for National Public Radio. He taught at Bennington College, Columbia University, Sarah Lawrence College, the University of Pennsylvania, and elsewhere. In 1990 he was the first creative writer appointed to the Abrams Chair of Jewish Studies at the University of Notre Dame. The recipient of grants from the National Endowment for the Arts and the New York State CAPS, he was visiting professor of creative writing at the State University of New York, Stony Brook. He died in 1997.

MARK RUDMAN was born in New York City and grew up in the midwest and west. He has received the Academy of American Poets Prize, the *Denver Quarterly* Award, the Max Hayward Award from PEN Columbia for his translation of Boris Pasternak's *My Sister—My Life*, fellowships in poetry from the Ingram Merrill Foundation, the New York Foundation on the Arts, the National Endowment for the Arts, and the Guggenheim Foundation. He has published nine books, most recently *Provoked in Venice*, and his poems have appeared in over 150 magazines and anthologies, including *Atlantic Monthly, Harper's, New Republic*, and the *New Yorker*, and *Literature: The Evolving Canon, After Ovid,* and *Best American Poetry and Essays*. His translations of poets such as Johannes Bobrowski, Rene Char, Ivan Drach, and his ongoing Horatian Palimpsests have been anthologized. His book *Rider* received the 1994 National Book Critics' Circle Award for Poetry. He teaches at New York University.

ELAINE TERRANOVA is a graduate of Temple University, where she has taught creative writing and literature. Her poems have appeared in the *New Yorker, American Poetry Review, Boulevard, Christian Science Monitor, Village Voice*, and other literary periodicals, and in her three books: *The Cult of the Right Hand, Toward Morning/Swimmers*, and most recently *Damages*. She was the 1996 Margaret Banister Writer in Residence at Sweet Briar College and has been workshop leader at the Chautauqua Institution, the Geraldine R. Dodge Poetry Festival, and the Rutgers Summer Writers' Conference. *Cult of the Right Hand* won the Academy of American Poets Walt Whitman Award for a first book. She has also received the Anna Davidson Rosenberg Award, in addition to grants and fellowships from Bread Loaf Writer's Conference, Pew Fellowships in the Arts, and Pennsylvania Council on the Arts.

KATHARINE WASHBURN is coeditor of the 1200-page *World Poetry: An Anthology of Verse from Antiquity Through Our Time*, translator of *Paul Celan: Last Poems*, and coeditor of *Dumbing Down*. She has received a grant from the National Endowment for the Arts and served for four years as an NEA panelist. Her novel *The Translator's Apology* will be published in 1998.